My wife always says if you want a relationship with no change, get a cat. If you married a person, read this book.

> —JOHN ORTBERG
> Pastor and Author
> Menlo Park Presbyterian Church

Change is inevitable—especially in marriage. That's why *Your Spouse Isn't the Person You Married* is so valuable. If you want to learn the secrets to navigating the ins and outs of your ever-changing marriage, you've got to read this book. It's practical, engaging, and grounded. Don't miss out its valuable message.

> —DRS. LES AND LESLIE PARROTT
> Founders of RealRelationships.com
> Authors of *Trading Places* and *Love Talk*

The Reissers truly understand the dynamics of shifting marriage relationships and how to weather the storms of life's change. Note to young couples—get this book now and save yourself marriage-counseling bills later.

> —GARY SMALLEY
> Author of *From Anger to Intimacy*

Your Spouse
isn't the person
You Married

KEEPING LOVE STRONG THROUGH LIFE'S CHANGES

TERI K. REISSER, MFT
PAUL C. REISSER, MD

Tyndale House Publishers, Inc.
CAROL STREAM, ILLINOIS

A Focus on the Family book published by Tyndale House Publishers, Inc., Carol Stream, Illinois 60188

Focus on the Family and the accompanying logo and design are federally registered trademarks of Focus on the Family, Colorado Springs, CO 80995.

TYNDALE and Tyndale's quill logo are registered trademarks of Tyndale House Publishers, Inc.

All Scripture quotations, unless otherwise indicated, are taken from the *Holy Bible, New International Version®*. NIV®. Copyright © 1973, 1978, 1984 by International Bible Society. Used by permission of Zondervan Publishing House. All rights reserved. Scripture quotations marked (KJV) are taken from the King James Version.

The case examples presented in this book are fictional composites based on the authors' clinical experience with hundreds of clients and patients through the years. Any resemblance between these fictional characters and actual persons is coincidental.

Editor: Marianne Hering
Cover design by Ron Kaufmann
Cover photograph by Stephen Vosloo. Copyright © 2009 by Tyndale House Publishers, Inc. All rights reserved.

The authors are represented by the literary agency of Alive Communications, Inc., 7680 Goddard Street, Suite 200, Colorado Springs, CO 80920, www.alivecommunications.com.

Library of Congress Cataloging-in-Publication Data
Reisser, Teri K.
  Your spouse isn't the person you married / Teri K. Reisser and Paul C. Reisser.
    p. cm.
  "A Focus on the Family book."
  Includes bibliographical references and index.
  ISBN 978-1-58997-547-7 (alk. paper)
  1. Marriage—Religious aspects—Christianity. 2. Change—Religious aspects—Christianity.
I. Reisser, Paul C. II. Focus on the Family (Organization) III. Title.
  BV835.R45 2010
  248.8'44019—dc22

                                    2009041238

ISBN: 978-1-58997-547-7

Printed in the United States of America
1 2 3 4 5 6 7 8 9 / 15 14 13 12 11 10

This book is dedicated to the hundreds of clients and patients who have trusted us enough to share their innermost hopes and fears. This decision to be so vulnerable never ceases to humble us, and we consider that trust to be sacred. We have ached with you in your trials and rejoiced with you in your victories.

Thank you for allowing us to walk with you.

Teri K. Reisser, MFT

Paul C. Reisser, MD

Contents

Introduction

You read the cover correctly.

Your spouse isn't the person you married—even if your wedding was yesterday (in fact, *especially* if your wedding was yesterday). Why? Because your spouse is a living, breathing, and thus *changing* human being. Keeping up with all of the ways he or she is changing and growing over the years is an incredibly satisfying process. Indeed, it's the very essence of intimacy, of knowing and being known by another person. It's even more satisfying than sex and, in turn, makes sex much more satisfying. On the flip side, *not* knowing your spouse and who he or she is becoming can take your marriage places you never wanted it to go.

We believe that couples can benefit from reading this book* whether their marriage is new or old, in full bloom or starting to wilt a little, a mighty fortress or in urgent need of repair. We also believe that this book will help people who would like to be married someday or who have a wedding looming in the near future. Indeed, if you're planning your nuptials and are taking time to read this book, congratulations. You're a few steps ahead of other soon-to-be newlyweds who are up to their eyeballs in wedding preparations and surging hormones, blissfully unaware of anything that might go wrong with *their* happily-ever-after. Last, but certainly not least, we've written this book for those

---

* Usually women pick up books about marriage because they tend to have emotional titles and covers that look like cosmetic ads instead of things that attract men, such as explosions or women in various states of undress.

who used to be married and aren't sure what went wrong, or those who are getting ready for a second or third try and don't want a repeat performance of the previous sad tale(s).

Don't get us wrong. We're not pessimistic about marriage. We've been married (to each other) for more than 30 years, and we really like how our life together has turned out. We're also firmly convinced that a safe and sane marriage benefits body, mind, and soul, as well as children, future generations, the community, the economy, and indeed, the welfare of an entire culture.

We also think that we have something to contribute to this subject. We've logged a lot of hours—as a marriage and family therapist (Teri) and a family physician (Paul)—counseling people in differing states of marital bliss and nonbliss. Many whom we have counseled through distress and crisis have found their marriages improved or even saved, at least that's what they said. We'd love to take credit for all of the good results, but we won't, mainly because we'd also have to take the blame for the train wrecks and flameouts. Even those who have persisted in dismantling their marriages, in spite of our best efforts, have provided some illuminating cautionary tales for this book.

A few disclaimers

While we sincerely hope that you'll find this book helpful, we also need to issue a few disclaimers and friendly reminders. These are important, so don't glaze over on us here.

Disclaimer no. 1. We've written much of this book describing a common marital arc: wed during the 20s, 2.5 children by age 30, and so forth. We're well aware that this picture doesn't apply to many couples, but to avoid writing a 10-volume tome, we haven't attempted to describe every possible marital theme and variation. (We have, however, addressed some common issues that arise in remarriages in "Appendix: Change in the Blended Family.") Nevertheless, the basic principles and observations in this book can be applied to nearly every marriage.

Disclaimer no. 2. Don't expect a quick fix from reading this (or any other) book. You might get a flash of insight that could prove to be a turning point in your life and/or marriage. But you still have to work out the details in "the dailies," those hour-by-hour events and responsibilities in life and relationships where your own rubber meets the road.

Disclaimer no. 3. This book isn't a substitute for good counseling, but it's probably a lot better than bad (or no) counseling. It will, however, probably provide some food for thought for discussions both inside and outside the counseling room. If your marriage needs a lot of work, a counselor who takes the time to hear your story and who knows what he or she is doing will definitely help you make progress.

Disclaimer no. 4. The stories we tell are drawn from real people and all-too-common scenarios, but as they used to say on the 1950s–1960s TV show *Dragnet*, the names and details have been changed to protect the innocent—and also to comply with HIPAA regulations.*

---

* HIPAA stands for the Health Insurance Portability and Accountability Act of 1996, an important federal law that, among other things, forbids health-care providers and counselors from disclosing confidential information to people who shouldn't read it, such as in-laws, telemarketers, and tabloid reporters.

Disclaimer no. 5. The "homework" assignments you'll find in some chapters weren't put there to fatten the page count. When you come across one of these, take out a pen and paper, or fire up your computer, and get to work. These assignments aren't a cookbook-style relationship recipe or fill-in-the-blanks fluff, by the way. Every marriage is a unique civilization, and taking time to do some thinking and writing about your specific circumstances is definitely a good idea.

Disclaimer no. 6. But seriously . . . Though we've injected some humor throughout this book, we're well aware that the fallout from marital stagnation or turbulence is anything but funny. The process that turns "I do" into "I don't anymore" is definitely unpleasant. When disillusion with a marriage partner leads to dissolution of a marriage, the pain is intense, the tears are abundant, the wounds are deep, and the scars are permanent. You may not want to hear this, but children— even adult children—generally don't weather their parents' divorce well. No matter how amicably the details may appear to be settled, there will still be long-term—indeed, lifelong—effects. (Obviously, we aren't in favor of keeping children or spouses in situations that are dangerous or abusive. In such cases, the first order of business is to ensure everyone's safety.) Bottom line: If your marriage is in trouble and you're hurting, we get it. We hope that you'll find comfort along with helpful advice in these pages, and perhaps a laugh or two along the way will help.

Prelude

We've been to a lot of weddings.

We've attended most of our friends' weddings and a good number of their kids' weddings. We've been to ceremonies where we've been excited about the impending union, and to others where we've cringed through the "let no man tear asunder" part because we knew enough about the bride and groom to be convinced that "asunder" would be coming sooner or later.

We've sung at more than a few weddings for family and friends and served as musical hired hands at a number of ceremonies for people we didn't know. We've tried to emote our way through songs we couldn't stand or to be heard over some impressive ambient noise at outdoor ceremonies. We can perform Paul Stookey's "The Wedding Song" in our sleep.

We've seen ceremonies that appeared to be on autopilot and others that were wonderfully creative. We've been to a few weddings where we wondered, "Why didn't *we* think of that?" and a few others where we groaned, "What were they thinking?"

Whatever the setup, the common denominator at all of these weddings has been unquenchable optimism, expressed not just in vows at the altar but also in tributes and toasts, in smiles and kisses in response to tinkling glasses, in dancing and bouquet tossing and whatever other customs the bride and groom have chosen to celebrate.

Weddings sometimes remind us of political conventions, where the prevailing mood is "everything will be wonderful once our candidate, who can leap tall buildings in a single bound, is elected." Even if we support the candidate, we know that he or she can't turn water into wine, and that everyday realities will bear down before the sun sets on the first day in office. Like the party nominee, the bride and groom are endowed with invincibility while basking in the heady limelight of cheers and congratulatory speeches. We watch the festivities and listen to the predictions of unending wedded bliss, knowing full well that the guests and the DJ will go home, the tuxes will go back to the shop, the flowers will wilt, the makeup will come off, and everyday clothes will go on. The honeymoon will be over, often well before it actually ends.

Change is coming

Who's That Sleeping in My Bed?

> For most people, a life lived alone, with passing strangers or passing lovers, is incoherent and ultimately unbearable. Someone must be there to know what we have done for those we love.
>
> —Psychiatrist and author Frank Pittman,
> *Psychology Networker*, March/April 2002

> It is not your love that sustains the marriage, but from now on, the marriage that sustains your love.
>
> —Pastor and theologian Dietrich Bonhoeffer,
> "A Wedding Sermon from a [Nazi] Prison Cell," May 1943

"Why did you get married?" might sound like a sappy conversation starter for a talk-show emcee or a wedding-shower hostess. But whether you've been married for 30 days or 30 years, it's actually an important question. The excitement and fervor that propelled you to the altar may now seem like a long-faded memory as you gaze upon the person snoring in your bed—the person who wears your ring but doesn't seem particularly attractive or interesting anymore. You may have spent more than one sleepless night (the snoring didn't help) wondering, *Why in the world did I get married? What was I thinking? Who* is *this person, anyway?* These and other anguish-filled questions may now be propelling you toward a rendezvous that you should definitely reconsider—such as with a lover who isn't your spouse, or even with a divorce lawyer.

What happened after the church emptied, the reception guests departed, the honeymoon suite was vacated, and the bride was carried across the threshold?* If you're not as excited about being married now as you were on your wedding day, what went wrong? Believe it or not, one of many possible strategies to find out (and to do something about it) involves revisiting the events and emotions of your premarital relationship. In this chapter we'll ask you to think carefully about what happened during those early days. Those memories may help you understand what's happening now, when things may not seem exciting and satisfying.

So to repeat the question: Why *did* you get married?

---

* The ancient tradition of the husband carrying his new bride across the threshold of their first home has a kind of Cary Grant old-movie charm to it, but its origins are somewhat less romantic. Once upon a time it was apparently considered bad luck if the bride stumbled while making the crossing, so presumably she would be safer being carried—unless, of course, the husband tripped, which would no doubt guarantee double misfortune (starting with two orthopedic bills).

Falling in love

People enter marriages for all kinds of reasons—physical attraction, verbal chemistry, shared values, common interests, emotional neediness, a financial upgrade, escape from an abusive situation, an unplanned pregnancy, even compatible horoscope signs. Some of these reasons are definitely more healthy and rational than others. But *most* people get married after experiencing something generally referred to as "falling in love." For centuries authors, poets, and songwriters have rhapsodized about this event. Fortunes have been made and lost because of it. Its power is undeniable. But keep in mind that much of being in love with someone actually involves *being in love with the way the other person makes you feel about yourself.*

Consider, for example, the lyrics to a few vintage love songs, such as the old favorite "You Are My Sunshine" *("You make me happy when skies are gray"),* or "You Light Up My Life," or even James Brown's raucous "I Got You (I Feel Good)." Although contemporary songwriters have stopped crooning about moons and Junes (and often tell ex-lovers what complete jerks they have been), the golden oldies express a powerful emotional response that usually happens in the early stages of a romance.

In the beginning, it's likely that your spouse-to-be thought you were the best-looking, funniest, deepest, kindest human on the face of the earth. Perhaps he gave you various tokens of proof that you were never far from his thoughts: flowers, cards (paper or the e-mail kind), Frappuccinos, text messages, or even those giant metallic balloons that remain inflated and clutter up your living space for a couple of months. She may have convinced you that no man had ever emotionally touched her like you had.

Every interaction conveyed how much she adored you. You were both working overtime to come up with creative ways to delight each other. You were content to shut out the rest of the world, and it seemed that you needed nothing except one another. All of your needs for human interaction were being met, oh so blissfully, by your newfound love. (Your friends may well have rolled their eyes and wondered where you had gone.)

If you've been married for a while, you're probably well aware that your relationship with your spouse doesn't involve nonstop emotional and physical ecstasy. Were those magical premarital times a fantasy that evaporated forever once the honeymoon was over? Not entirely. More likely than not, they involved the development of *intimacy* (and we're not actually speaking of the physical kind)—something we desperately want and need as human beings. We will enter into a marriage because we're convinced we've found (or will find) this precious commodity in our relationship with our beloved. Sadly, far too many marriages unravel because one or both partners decide that intimacy is beckoning from a nonmarital relationship.

Dallas Willard, author and philosophy professor extraordinaire at USC (but that's forgivable even by Paul, who graduated from UCLA School of Medicine), has described intimacy as "the mutual mingling of souls who are taking each other into themselves to ever increasing depths."[1] We're likely to take our first steps toward a "mutual mingling" of souls in the beginning of a romantic relationship, when a positive feedback loop is readily set in motion:

1. Two people are mutually attracted to each other.
2. Each responds to the other in a way that says, "You are absolutely perfect!" This may be based on complete naïveté,

on temporary blindness to the other's imperfections, or even on viewing some otherwise annoying behaviors as engaging.*

3. Bathed in this reciprocal glowing opinion, each is authentically desirous of knowing more about, and being known more by, the other person. The motivation to spend time with the other person, and to know more about the other, is genuine and natural. (We're assuming that the two people are/were actually interested in each other and not faking or calculating their moves primarily to serve some ulterior motive—such as getting sex or money, making someone else jealous, getting a promotion, etc. Though our motives in life and love are rarely pure, or even clear to ourselves, the existence of genuine mutual attraction will be our working premise for this chapter.)

4. The more the other person is persistent, consistent, thoughtful, and meticulous in attentiveness, the more cared for and deeply loved each feels.

5. The more loved and cared for each feels, the greater is the incentive to serve the other in response.

6. In this gloriously untested state of rapport, the relationship is idealized, because flaws have yet to be divulged, discovered, or acknowledged. Each has finally found the "perfect" person. It's much like the feeling we have when we first lay eyes on our newborn child: No matter what imperfection declares itself to our eyes, our hearts insist that here is a *perfect* human being.

---

* Paul's father had a number of favorite quips, including this one about romantic naïveté: "Love is blind, but marriage is a real eye-opener!"

Though we may be describing this courtship process with a little tongue in the old cheek, the joyous drive to know and be known by another person resonates with our deepest emotional needs. The experience of feeling accepted and cared for uncritically evokes powerful feelings of safety. We can (perhaps for the first time in our lives) let down our guard and relax into the literal sanctuary of a relationship in which anxiety about our self-worth is banished. This is the long-yearned-for place where we sense that another human being knows us thoroughly, warts and all. (God, through His omnipotence and love, is the only one who can *truly* know us. What we mean here is the best knowing that's humanly possible, which is still a wonderful and deep experience.)

A person who has put the effort into knowing you has made a profound summary judgment: "I'm believing the best in you, and I'm with you—not only now but for the rest of our lives. Even when you screw up, I won't jump to conclusions and judge you, but I'll always see you in the best possible light." If we are known thoroughly (including all of our flaws and points of deepest shame) and are still treasured by at least one other person, then we aren't alone in the world. The great existential terror—*What if my life has no significance?*—is exorcised.

A witnessed life

At the Reisser house, we regularly find wonderful illustrations of important truths about marriage (and life in general) in films we've enjoyed—or endured. One night we were surprised to find some powerful dialogue in an otherwise so-so film. The protagonist, John Clark (played by Richard Gere), is vaguely discontented with his life, though not with his 19-year marriage. He discovers that dancing lessons seem to fill this void, but he doesn't want to inform his wife about this new passion—not because he's cheating on her, but because he's concerned that revealing it would hurt her feelings. When his unexplained absences arouse some concern, his wife, Beverly, hires a private detective, who in short order discovers John's secret. Once she finds out, Beverly dismisses the detective during a conversation that broaches the question, "Why do people get married?" This is her profound reply:

> We need a witness to our lives. There are a billion people on the planet. I mean, what does any one life really mean? But in a marriage, you're promising to care about everything. The good things, the bad things, the terrible things, the mundane things. All of it, all of the time, every day. You're saying, "Your life will not go unnoticed because *I* will notice it. Your life will not go unwitnessed because *I* will be your witness."[2]

One of the biggest mistakes any young couple can make is thinking that the task of "knowing" the other person has been accomplished, and that his or her thoughts and behavior will be entirely predictable for the next 50 years. There are two big—and inescapable—realities of life that will ensure these naive assumptions won't come to pass.

Big reality no. 1: The dailies

The first big reality of life is something we call "the dailies," and they won't be ignored. These are the repetitive, and oh-so-daily, tasks required to earn a living, set up housekeeping, put food on the table, raise children, and so on. Our blissful couple returns from the honeymoon to find that bills need to be paid, degrees need to be finished, and careers need to be launched. The in-laws may also feel a "need" to help rule the couple's new little civilization. Suddenly the intensely protected bubble of "us" bursts before an onslaught of the demands of daily living. The newlyweds dutifully begin dealing with financial necessities and social obligations. They eventually settle into a routine that may—or may not—include some time alone together. A pregnancy is happily announced. The extended families are so pleased. The couple is pleased that everyone is pleased. Everything is on schedule, including trouble on the horizon.

With the addition of a couple of kids, our no-longer-newlyweds are well on their way toward establishing a lifestyle that lacks margin and breathing room. (We'll have more to say about that subject in chapter 4.) The husband is getting anxious: Not only did he fail to make his first million by age 30, but he's beginning to feel as if he *owes* a million instead. *How on earth can we afford the mortgage payment on a bigger house?* The wife may be playing the "we have the most perfect home and marriage" game with her friends while her brain is grappling with a nagging but increasingly insistent question—*Is this what I signed on for? I used to have my own life—what happened to* my *plans?* More likely than not, she's exhausted for a number of reasons, including sleep deprivation when her children are infants and (a few years later) when the demands of her kids' schedules turn her into a chauffeur, hurtling in her SUV back and forth to school, lessons, games, practices, and birthday parties.

The days of wine, roses, and (most important) those "I'm all ears" conversations are long gone. There's no time or energy for the little acts of kindness and generosity that once fueled romantic feelings and actions. Sex that previously included candles, music, playfulness, and excitement has become a painful source of vague but increasing resentment on both sides of the bed. The temperature of the relationship has shifted from the warm glow of finding new ways to delight each other to the stony chill of maintaining a mental account of ever-accruing disappointments. Husband and wife fall into bed each night utterly exhausted, their conversation limited to details about schedules, finances, problem solving, and, all too often, the argument du jour.

Big reality no. 2: Stuff happens

As the years go by, all kinds of stuff—good and bad—happens, and as a result your life changes in more ways than you may care to count. More important, *you change, and so does the person to whom you are married.* All of these changes can affect the health and stability of your marriage, for better or (far too often) for worse. Later in this book we're going to take a more detailed look at a number of these areas of change and the ways they impact a marriage. For the moment, however, consider the following question, and see if any of the answers apply to you.

How do you and your spouse change? Let us count the ways.

Change no. 1—physically. As we watch birthday candles accumulate every year, our bodies begin to notify us that certain parts don't look or work as well as they used to. Multiple areas of the anatomy begin to sag, enlarge, or shrink. Much of this occurs through the normal passage of years and decades, but a lot of unwelcome change comes about through everyday habits. Most people become more "fuel efficient" in their middle- and late-adult years, but few actually reduce their food intake. The human body interprets this as saving for a rainy day (or a whole lot of them), and fat will dutifully accrue, resulting in the proverbial spare tire or an expanding aft section. Lack of exercise and other unwise habits (inhaling or chewing tobacco, drinking alcohol to excess, abusing various chemical substances, etc.) accelerate undesirable physical changes. Untold billions of dollars are spent every year on supplements, surgeries, and other services intended to slow or even reverse the wages of aging. But time will have its way with us and our spouses alike, and it may bring other unwelcome guests, including chronic or life-threatening disease.

Most wedding vows include pledges to love, honor, and cherish the other person in sickness and in health, but few young couples standing at the altar have seriously contemplated the scenario of caring for a spouse who is chronically ill, bedridden, or demented. Sadly, long before that moment arrives, many marriages begin to unravel because one member—usually, but not always, the husband—becomes fixated on physical appearance and develops wandering eyeballs (and other body parts) when a spouse's frame starts to show some wear and tear. All too often the man, in particular, has gone looking for a newer model when the bride of his youth has aged, gracefully or not, often bearing permanent changes from carrying his children. This destructive and futile quest is often propelled by the wife's loss of interest in sex, a development that is predictable and usually repairable but poorly understood by either spouse. (We'll have much more to say on that subject in chapter 5.)

Change no. 2—emotionally, intellectually, spiritually. We mark our milestones, celebrate our accomplishments, regret our mistakes, and grieve our losses. We read a book that prompts a subtle adjustment in our thought processes. We hear a speaker who challenges our assumptions. We struggle with the wisdom or practicality of our politics. We're forced to face our limitations and alter our positions. We realize our values have shifted. We have some experiences that we can't sort into neat categories. We find that some issues in life are more complicated than we thought, and others we make more complicated than they need to be. Some of our formulas for understanding ourselves, other people, and the world around us need to be revisited, updated, upgraded, deepened, widened, or perhaps rethought entirely. We may enter marriage with a mature and active relationship with God—or one that is stale, perfunctory, or nonexistent. We may meet God for the first time after our wedding day or experience a crisis of faith when something goes terribly wrong in our lives or the life of a loved one.

So who is the most logical person in the world to hear the download of these evolving thoughts and feelings? If you're married, the correct answer is "the beautiful soul mate for whom I would have sailed to the ends of the earth years ago!" And yet all too often this doesn't happen. Why? We'll explore that all-important question, and what to do about it, in the next chapter.

Change no. 3—people in your life. Sixteenth-century English poet and preacher John Donne spoke the famous words, "No man is an island," to which we would add this not-so-famous observation: "No marriage is an island either." People will come in and out of your life as individuals and couples, and you won't be the same as a result. The family in which you grew up—your *family of origin*—significantly shaped how you think and react, and usually will continue to do so after you're married. If you have one or more children, they will profoundly and permanently change your life. Your relationships with friends, acquaintances, co-workers, even pets will also affect you and your marriage. In a best-case scenario, they all can be part of a rich, life-enhancing tapestry. In a worst-case scenario, they can be a source of nonstop drama, heartache, chaos, and emotional exhaustion. The worst-case scenario, however, is alienation and isolation from spouse, kids, extended family, the world at large, and ultimately, God.

Change no. 4—financially. During your courtship you may have been convinced that you could live on love, and money wouldn't be that big a deal. As current events spectacularly confirm, for most of us the state of our finances will definitely change over time. Whether we gain or lose (or do a fair amount of each), the flow of money in and out of our accounts can either enhance or undermine our marriage. (More on this topic in chapter 6.)

Change no. 5—gains and losses. Over the course of our lives, we all experience gains and losses—or at least what would seem to be so at face value. Most of us would consider these things on the gain side: a loving family, a stable marriage, children and grandchildren, an education to whatever level we can attain, a meaningful and satisfying vocation, friendships, a nice home and things to fill it, vacation travel, and long-standing good health. And most of us would definitely place an unstable upbringing, one or more turbulent marriages, disruptive and dissolute children (or none at all), catastrophic financial losses or outright poverty, unemployment, isolation, disease, and an early grave in the minus column. We all seek to maximize gain and minimize loss as we understand them, but the reality is that every life is composed of an ongoing blend of these entities.

This might sound like a pronouncement from the little-known superhero Captain Obvious (who has long been a fixture in the Reisser family, usually invoked by a film with poor writing), but many of us live—and enter marriage—with profound assumptions about how life *should* be and/or even more profound fears about losses we desperately want to avoid. When we suffer a major loss, most of us ask, "Why me?" as if we expect to exit this life without experiencing any serious reversals. Here's a news flash: *Every life, and every marriage, will experience losses, and losses will bring about change.* Sadly, big losses—especially the ones that everyone dreads, such as a calamity involving a child—often lead to the unraveling of a marriage. Surprisingly, events that might seem like major gains for husband or wife may put a marriage in jeopardy as well.

Change no. 6—seasons of life. Often on a parallel track with gains and losses are certain seasons of life that are predictable but still manage to catch many couples by surprise. For men, these are often work related. Early career ambitions can generate extreme work hours and drive wedges between husbands and their wives, and between fathers and their children. Promotions, relocations, reorganizations, and layoffs all rearrange the marital furniture. Disillusionment with the rewards of achievement ("I worked my hind quarters off for *this?*") or failure to reach an elusive brass ring can provoke a literal off-the-deep-end midlife crisis. Retirement may have beckoned like a long-awaited entry into an earthly paradise, but the actual event may prove to be disappointing and underfunded; it may also lead to an identity crisis of sorts *(If I'm not marketing widgets, how do I define myself?).*

For women, the seasons of life frequently relate to the bearing, rearing, and eventual launching of children into adulthood. If a woman has an educational or career track in progress, it will almost certainly be altered by the responsibilities of child rearing, sometimes to a drastic degree. Women who embrace motherhood as a primary calling may nonetheless wonder about their identity, especially when the children are small and require virtual 24-7 on-call attention, or when they leave the nest. Dr. James Dobson has recounted a conversation with his wife, Shirley, that occurred as Focus on the Family was rapidly growing. He was becoming a nationally recognized speaker and author while she stayed home with two young children. "I know who you are," she observed at the end of a particularly trying day, "but who am I?" That question would partly be answered soon after her youngest left the nest, when she became chair of the National Day of Prayer in 1991. But for many wives, the answer to the "Who am I?" question may generate considerable personal and marital turbulence, especially if it's never clearly recognized and addressed.

Note to couples who don't fit the aforementioned description: We fully understand that every couple's seasons are different, that children may not enter the marital equation, or that Dad may stay at home with the kids while Mom is the primary breadwinner. There are always exceptions, but the scenarios we've sketched are definitely the most common.

Weathering changes

How will your marriage weather these (and other) changes? Actually, the question should be, How is your marriage weathering these changes *now?* (since, like it or not, they *are* happening). Hopefully it is faring well—not merely intact but enhanced through resilience, preventive maintenance, and personal growth. But far less satisfying outcomes are all too common, even among couples who begin their marriages with the most fervent passion for each other and commitment to the permanence of their union before God—"till death do us part." If your marriage is showing some definite signs of wear or is coming unglued, you need to understand what has happened and begin the repair work *now.* If you're not experiencing any apparent strain at the moment, good for you—but you should commit to intentional weatherproofing that will be ongoing (meaning for the rest of your life).

In the next few chapters we're going to offer a guided tour of the foundations that must be laid, reinforced, or possibly rebuilt if you want your marriage to survive and thrive through the twists and turns of life. If you've read a book or two about marriage or ventured forth to a couples' retreat, you may feel as if you've had your fill of advice about some topics, such as improving communication with your spouse, repairing your self-image, or understanding how your upbringing affects your marriage, to name a few. Point taken, but this stuff continues to drive people into the counseling office—it's that important, and yet it's poorly handled by far too many couples.

Then, in chapters 7 through 10, we'll take a look at a number of common, important, and often predictable life events that are definite change agents. Aside from keeping counselors busy, these change agents also guarantee that you and your spouse are not and will not be the same people who stood at the altar however many months or years ago.

That isn't necessarily bad, by the way. Change is a sign of life. You can prepare for it, embrace it, and most important, grow through it.

Better yet, you and your spouse can grow *closer* through it and experience what nineteenth-century English poet Robert Browning wrote in this famous line: "Grow old along with me! The best is yet to be."[3]

Exercise: So you think you know your spouse?

Let's find out how well you know your spouse. Answer the following questions twice—once for yourself, and a second time as you think your spouse will answer. Answer either yes or no. You'll be exasperated with some of the items, but try not to qualify your answers; just put whichever answer seems most accurate. After you have each finished, sit down and compare your responses. Give yourself a point for every time you correctly guessed what your spouse would answer. Are either of you surprised by who got the higher score?

Valentine's Day is very important
to me.   You: _____   Your spouse: _____

I enjoy watching the World Series.   You: _____   Your spouse: _____

I would adopt if we couldn't
have children.   You: _____   Your spouse: _____

Hair left in the shower bothers me.   You: _____   Your spouse: _____

I'd just as soon skip church.   You: _____   Your spouse: _____

I like having friends and family
gather at our house.   You: _____   Your spouse: _____

I rarely exceed the speed limit.   You: _____   Your spouse: _____

I feel comfortable discussing sex
with my spouse.   You: _____   Your spouse: _____

Credit-card balances should be paid
off monthly.   You: _____   Your spouse: _____

There is a correct way to hang a roll
    of toilet paper.   You: ____   Your spouse: ____

I am an impulsive spender.   You: ____   Your spouse: ____

The best vacation is doing nothing
    at the beach.   You: ____   Your spouse: ____

I like having my own scissors, tape,
    and stapler.   You: ____   Your spouse: ____

I would rather be cremated than
    buried.   You: ____   Your spouse: ____

I prefer French cooking over Italian. You: ____   Your spouse: ____

I feel guilty if I'm not being productive. You: ____   Your spouse: ____

White and dark clothing should be
    separated before washing.   You: ____   Your spouse: ____

Men should put down the seat after
    using the toilet.   You: ____   Your spouse: ____

Borrowing money from family is
    acceptable.   You: ____   Your spouse: ____

The stay-at-home parent should
    work after the children are grown. You: ____   Your spouse: ____

I am an excellent listener.   You: ____   Your spouse: ____

My spouse is an excellent listener. You: ____   Your spouse: ____

My favorite date is dinner and
    a movie.   You: ____   Your spouse: ____

I could accept an openly homosexual
    couple attending my church.   You: ____   Your spouse: ____

Spouses can have separate checking
    accounts.   You: ____   Your spouse: ____

Prayer is an important part of my life. You: ____   Your spouse: ____

Holidays should be spent with the extended family.	You: _____	Your spouse: _____
I prefer comedy to drama movies.	You: _____	Your spouse: _____
When I get angry, I need time before I can talk.	You: _____	Your spouse: _____
It is never okay to drink excessively.	You: _____	Your spouse: _____
Gross jokes offend me.	You: _____	Your spouse: _____
I would move to advance my spouse's career.	You: _____	Your spouse: _____
I eat four or more servings of fruits and veggies daily.	You: _____	Your spouse: _____
I am more of a leader than a follower.	You: _____	Your spouse: _____
My sex drive is the same as when we met.	You: _____	Your spouse: _____
I believe household chores are to be split 50-50.	You: _____	Your spouse: _____
We have enough life insurance.	You: _____	Your spouse: _____
TOTALS:	**You:** _____	**Your spouse:** _____

Endnotes

1. Dallas Willard, *The Divine Conspiracy* (San Francisco: HarperSanFrancisco, 1997), 163.
2. *Shall We Dance?* by Peter Chelsom (Miramax Films, 2004).
3. Robert Browing, "Rabbi Ben Ezra," *The Works of Robert Browning* (Hertfordshire, England: Wordsworth Editions, 1999), 1:481.

2

Do You Know What Your Spouse Is Thinking About?

> If you could read my mind, love,
> What a tale my thoughts could tell . . .
>
> —Gordon Lightfoot, "If You Could Read My Mind"

Do not under any circumstances skip this chapter!

In the last chapter we listed a slew of everyday events that can bring about shifts in our thoughts and feelings. Some of these can emerge quickly, whereas others may hatch over months or even years. (Go back to "Big reality no. 2: Stuff happens" in chapter 1 if you don't remember our examples.) We then raised a critical question: So who is the most logical person in the world to hear the download of these evolving thoughts and feelings? If you're married, the correct answer is "The beautiful soul mate for whom I would have sailed to the ends of the earth years ago!" And yet all too often, this doesn't happen. Why?

Could you be the "last to know"?

Why could you be the last person to find out what's on your spouse's mind (or vice versa)? The answers to this question are so important that they launched the entire book, which is why you should listen up.

One reason is that we often don't have the time or opportunity to articulate to ourselves—much less anyone else—what exactly we're experiencing, thinking, and feeling. Our day-to-day schedules can be so hectic that they don't allow us time to think or reflect, and the adjustments we make often happen in such small increments that years may pass before we even understand how life has altered us.

Another reason that shifts in thought and feeling about important topics aren't revealed to a spouse is that one assumes, correctly or not, that the other person will become too unsettled—or panicked—over whatever is shared. *You want to change churches? You don't like your job? You don't want to spend Christmas with my parents? You've become a Democrat?*

Here's an important news flash: *We all desperately need someone to whom we can verbalize what's brewing inside our cranium, someone who will listen thoughtfully and carefully, without raised eyebrows, smirks, editorial comments, arguments, or threats.* And we'll draw very close to whoever serves this vital function, whether or not it's the person to whom we're married.

There's a third reason why your mate may not be up to speed with the changes you're experiencing, and it's important enough that it will be a recurring theme throughout this book. *Over the years, you may not have cultivated the intentional habit of keeping track of your spouse's ongoing thoughts and life experiences.* Here's a big red-flag warning: You can be around your spouse all day long, carrying on small talk and doing a decent job with the necessary business of running a household and/or earning a living, without ever accomplishing what we're talking about here. This kind of communication does *not* happen spontaneously. As we'll describe momentarily, it must be a deliberate, regular activity. But first, consider the story of John and Sallie:

> Married for about 15 years, John and Sallie have three children and successful careers. Sallie grew up in a family that took Catholicism *very* seriously, whereas John had no religious training during childhood. Sallie abandoned all church involvement in early adulthood. She and John became evangelical Christians several years into their marriage. (This was first instigated by Sallie, and John was satisfied to go in the same direction.) Though she hadn't been active in religious activities for years, Sallie's family of origin was very disappointed that she had re-embraced her spirituality via a Protestant church.
>
> She and John were active and involved in their church until a couple of years ago, when John began a reassessment of his faith life, which ultimately led him to the conclusion that the Catholic Church was the setting in which he could best feel God's presence. He didn't share his two years of soul searching and investigation with Sallie because he knew she wouldn't be open to re-embracing Catholicism. But Sallie also had no idea that John was in this soul-searching process because they had abandoned any semblance of a shared journey for the previous two decades.
>
> By the time she found out that he was even *on* a quest, he

had already enrolled in the catechism class required for precon-
verts. She felt betrayed and became more rigid in her stance,
unable to hear his (too-late) explanation as a genuine quest of his
soul. He in turn felt disrespected and marginalized. ("Wow—I
was happy to cooperate with her spiritual leanings for most of our
marriage. Why am I not allowed to explore now?") Though not
adept at sharing on a deep, intimate level, they are amicable and
join together for social times with friends and family. But as soon
as they're alone and the conversation turns serious, they dig in to
protect against the wounds that each is certain the other will
inflict.

The consequences of losing track

What happens when you lose track of what your spouse is thinking and
feeling? The short answer is "Plenty, and none of it is good," as Sallie and
John's story painfully illustrates. If you don't check in and do an attentive, respectful mutual download with your spouse on a regular basis,
you're likely to wake up one day and realize that you literally don't know,
and may not particularly like, the person to whom you're married.

You may sense that the other person hasn't been aware of your mental processing for the past several months—or years. You may slowly
erect a wall around your thoughts and emotions that says (with or without words), "I'm doing this myself; you don't understand me anymore."
If your spouse hasn't been there to hear the details and hasn't done the
work of keeping up with what you're thinking and feeling, you may
experience a sense of futility. *Why try to explain all of this now? It would*

be too big a project, and besides, I'm not sure you'd get it or even care about getting it. In fact, I'm not sure I even want you to get it at this point.

The importance of tracking the trajectory of your spouse's evolving thought life cannot be overstated. Opinions, worldviews, and values usually don't change overnight. They develop in tiny subterranean shifts of the soul as a person daily, weekly, monthly, and yearly adjusts to life's experiences. Most important, these shifts often happen unconsciously and therefore may not be verbalized. When two people sit down over coffee and intentionally allow time for each to find the words for what they're thinking about—a process that often involves a considerable amount of struggle, by the way—those preconscious wisps of feelings have a chance of being identified.

How aligned are your spiritual values?

Some couples meet at a local church or other group (such as a youth camp) with a spiritual context. Those who do meet this way usually enter marriage not only with a well-articulated understanding of their faith but also with a clear and purposeful spiritual unity. Typically they have decided that spiritual congruence is a prerequisite for any relationship that might lead to marriage. This is a wise course of action for many reasons, but not one that is universally followed. Indeed, too many married couples don't arrive at the altar with their religious values clearly articulated.

(continued)

Although differences of opinion about *religious* values (institutional beliefs and practices) may not seem too troublesome during the early bloom of a relationship, the significance of our spiritual convictions becomes increasingly apparent as the years pass. Many who read this book may be well versed in the content of the Bible and may have deep commitments to its teachings. What if your spouse doesn't share your views? Perhaps you knowingly married someone who doesn't share your faith, and now the seeds of spiritual discord are sprouting up as weeds. Perhaps you were both on the same page years ago as atheists or agnostics, and now one of you has made a fervent commitment to Jesus Christ. Perhaps you were both on the same page years ago as believers in Jesus Christ, but now you've got some different ideas about worship, music, or even some of the content you're hearing from the pulpit.

Here's a hot tip: Most couples get into trouble when discussing issues because they're more committed to winning than to actually understanding the other person's point of view, let alone giving it credence. Thus *it is vitally important that you and your spouse feel heard, understood, and respected when there is a difference of opinion regarding spiritual values.* Not only does this prevent discord and anger—which is what Scripture would ask of us, by the way—but from a practical standpoint you're more likely to succeed at wooing, rather than arguing, the other person to your viewpoint.

But if this regular download doesn't occur, the first time a person becomes aware of a change in a spouse's mind and heart may be when confronted with a behavior or announcement that arrives like a tsunami—unexpected, unheralded, and catastrophic. An exasperated question that erupts all too often in the counseling room is "If you've been this unhappy for 10 years, why didn't you *say* something so that I could have done something about it?" But often the partner hadn't clearly realized, let alone understood, what was brewing in his or her mind and heart for so long—and now a crisis is in full swing. At that point, chances of reconciliation are reduced because the gulf between spouses is now too great, and the person who was blindsided is drowning in feelings of betrayal and panic. *How did this happen? How did we go from celebrating our anniversary to this place? Why didn't he or she give me a heads-up? Why didn't I get a chance to be part of whatever was needed to prevent this from happening?*

Usually the answer is this: *The spouse who appears to have gone off the deep end wasn't necessarily deliberately withholding the various trains of thought that led to the marital earthquake.* Rather, changes evolved in such a way that the person undergoing the transformation wasn't fully aware of what was happening. It was experienced as vague anxiety and dissatisfaction with life, with an identification of the "exact cause" of this restlessness occurring only late in the game. The process of finding words to describe the turbulence and understand its causes should be accomplished with a carefully listening spouse. But all too often, someone outside the marriage with a sympathetic ear serves as the muse who helps a person find his or her voice. They then experience the emotional intimacy that follows.

The person lying beside you in bed night after night, year after year, is not the same individual who stood with you at the altar on your wedding day. Everyone changes. Everyone's worldview evolves because we are thinking, emotional creatures. It's naive and foolish to believe that the views, opinions, and values held by you or the person you married were cast in concrete on your wedding day. A wise spouse understands the critical importance of creating a scheduled and protected space on the calendar for the sole agenda of allowing the other person an opportunity to put into words what is currently incubating in the heart and mind.

Before we go much further with this train of thought, we need to acknowledge that there are many other reasons why this mutual, and indeed intimate, sharing of thoughts and feelings can become extinct:

- All too often a basic set of communication skills is never learned, and years of unresolved fights have left each person feeling hurt, unheard, and disrespected.
- Husband, wife, or both may become incredibly careless about treating the other person with basic courtesy.
- One or both spouses may have learned how to function in his or her own daily sphere of life without the other's input or understanding.
- A perpetually packed calendar reflects an overloaded, marginless lifestyle that effectively extinguishes these conversations, because one or both spouses are too busy, distracted, or tired to have them.

These aren't minor issues. In fact, they're so important and foundational that we're going to spend the next few chapters addressing them. It's critical to understand, however, that *a lapse in knowing and being known can occur even in marriages that are stable and congenial.* Couples who have enjoyed a long, stable marriage may have this situation sneak up on them because they *did* stay in touch for the first decade or so and then became complacent. While the loss of soul-to-soul intimacy may occur so gradually as to be unnoticed for years, it has the alarming potential to set up a scenario that can destroy a marriage—even one that has seemed solid for two or three decades—with breathtaking suddenness. Let's take a look at how that can happen.

The plot thickens . . . One day, a third person appears on the scene, often in a most innocent relationship. He or she may be a neighbor, a fellow employee, or perhaps a co-worker on a church committee. There may not be any physical attraction whatsoever, at least at first. The critical element of the scenario is *not* that this person is so appealing to the eye but rather that he or she is actually interested in who you are, what you think, and what you feel. This isn't someone with whom you have to do the dailies. You're not spending time dealing with strong-willed children, paying bills, making repairs, cleaning up dog poop, arguing about household chores, or struggling with the tax return. Even more important, you're not being judged, criticized, interrupted, or simply blown off while you're sharing your innermost thoughts and concerns. He or she isn't trying to "fix" you.

Instead, this person brings back everything that was wonderful about the courtship period with your spouse: the sense of endless and compassionate listening and the heady vibe that comes when another person is projecting, "Nothing is more important to me right now than listening to you." In addition, in this safe and uncritical place, you may be able to identify and find words for all of the vague discontent that has been gnawing at you. Everything starts making sense, including a revelation that your marriage isn't doing all that well. In fact, it may not take too much to convince you that your marriage is the *source* of whatever doesn't feel right in your life.

Eventually these conversations seem to feel like, to quote Dallas Willard again, "the mutual mingling of souls who are taking each other into themselves to ever increasing depths." In other words, they create emotional intimacy, which, more often than not, progresses to sexual intimacy. A sobering take-home warning is that this scenario, and the incredible heartbreak that follows, isn't confined to the Jerry Springer trash-talk crowd or the perpetual-emotion plots of daytime television. It happens to executives and stay-at-home moms, to teachers and doctors, to pastors, church staff, and members of elder boards. It happens in marriages where wedding vows were taken with the greatest sincerity, where moral values have been taught to children, where there have been longstanding commitments to honor and follow God. All of these can be cast aside, to the shock and dismay of family and friends (and at times, the general public), when involvement with a person outside of the marriage meets a desperate need that has been gnawing at the soul, perhaps for decades: Someone once again cares about what you're thinking and *feeling*.

Benefits of staying in touch

What happens when you remain in touch with (and engaged with) what your spouse is thinking and feeling? The short answer is "Plenty, and all of it is good." Taking the time to sit down or walk and talk with your spouse on a frequent basis to find out what he or she is feeling and thinking about benefits the marriage bond in three important ways.

First, it brings you up to speed on what is going on in the other person's mind. You have the latest news flashes, and you're also current on developing stories. You're less likely to hear a seismic announcement one day—such as "I've decided to become a Tibetan monk" or "I don't love you anymore; in fact, now that I've really thought about it, I never did love you"—without having a clue that some serious marital fault lines were forming.

Second, when you help someone put words to what is hatching inside him or her—and you don't judge, tell that person what he or she should (or shouldn't) feel, or immediately try to fix it—that person automatically draws closer to you because you listened so intently. (This is what happens in therapy, by the way.) Unfortunately, as we've just described, it can also happen at Starbucks or at some secluded rendezvous when someone else of the opposite sex (whose motives may not be exactly pure) does the listening and, in so doing, seems irresistibly understanding and attractive. If a person has experienced years of a spouse telling him or her *not* to feel a certain way, it can be intoxicating when someone comes along who is willing to listen and accept how he or she feels.

Third, if you've done a good job of listening, you have a golden opportunity to weave your own value system into what the other person is hatching. Try as you might, you can't dictate your spouse's value system, even if you're convinced beyond a doubt that you are right. But when you've listened without judgment or coercion, he or she will be more trusting of you, and more willing to consider *your* opinions and feelings. *Think about it:* In any sphere of life we're likely to be more willing to negotiate and reach a compromise with someone who makes an effort to understand—and especially respect—our point of view, as compared with someone who is simply trying to manipulate us into complying with his or her agenda.

Here's an example of the value of the checking-in process from our own recent history. There's a story involved, so bear with us. In 2008, we took our first-ever missions trip. (We're definitely late bloomers in this regard, but the right people and situation presented themselves, God gave the nudge, and off we went.) We spent several days working in a rural clinic in Uganda. Prior to our arrival, the ministry that operated the clinic ran announcements on a local radio station that an American physician (specifically, Paul) and two dentists would be seeing patients at no charge on three particular days.

Hundreds of people showed up with all sorts of problems: Acute infections, severe deformities, complications of HIV, depression, seizures, and chronic pain in every possible body part. We saw two rape cases. We saw a young woman with an aggressive pelvic tumor. We saw children who had lost parents, and we saw spouses who had lost partners to AIDS. Though staffed by competent and caring nurses, the clinic had very limited resources. All in all it was an eye-opening, educational, humbling, gratifying (occasionally), heartbreaking (most of the time), exhausting experience, somewhat like squaring off against a forest fire with a squirt gun. You could extinguish a twig here and there, while everything else was going up in flames. To top things off, at the end of the trip Teri became very ill.

As the plane took off for home, Paul felt thrashed, frustrated, and angry. Teri had made a promise to the ministry (without talking to Paul first) that we would be back every year until a new clinic was built. Paul, on the other hand, never wanted to set foot in Africa again. After a week of stewing at home (and when Teri had recovered from her sickness), Paul asked for a check-in time over dinner. Teri listened patiently while Paul worked through his feelings about returning to Uganda, the promise that had been made without his input, and the prospects of working in the clinic again. Her questions helped Paul identify what had bothered him so much about the experience. Paul in turn listened to Teri's thoughtful and heartfelt take on what we had accomplished. By the end of the dinner Paul had by no means signed on for another trip, but he felt understood and most of all *heard*.

Over the course of a year we had further conversations about Uganda. We agreed to return to the same ministry but with a different agenda: teach groups of pastors about marriage and help the clinic upgrade its services. This time there would be no forest-fire experience. That mission was accomplished in August 2009, though for Paul it proved to be another uphill battle. Teri experienced another illness at the end of the trip (though not as severe as the first time), and Paul wasn't completely exasperated on the way home. But once again there was a need to sit down after the trip and explore some issues. Teri has a calling, a heart for this work. For Paul, being in Africa pushes some deep-seated buttons related to safety, loss of control, and the need to "fix" things that can't be readily fixed (at least the way he would like). When meeting an orphan child with cerebral palsy, for example, Teri scooped her onto her lap for a cuddle session while Paul fretted about the little girl's medical problems that needed to be addressed and his lack of training and resources to do so. In another long conversation (after a week at home to regroup, as before), Teri helped Paul sort out what he found so hard about this trip, and Paul better understood why Teri felt it so worthwhile. Again, both felt heard and respected, and some new ideas were projected that might make any future trips a better experience.

We cannot overstate how these conversations helped each of us articulate the thoughts and feelings that were brewing within, while understanding the other's thoughts and feelings as well, about some very important issues. *This wasn't merely the result of Teri's being a good counselor* (which she is). It happened because we found the time to be unhurried and undistracted, and to hear the other person out without interruption. We acknowledged that we were coming from different places, and that neither of us was wrong or unreasonable for what we were feeling. Neither person was trying to fix the other. But in the process we definitely got up to speed on each other's thoughts, we drew closer, and we found ways to weave together what we care (and worry) about in the ongoing project of helping our friends in Uganda.

What will happen in 2010? Stay tuned.

Staying in touch

How do you stay in touch with your spouse? We strongly urge couples to commit to a regularly scheduled, look-me-in-the-eye conversation session that we refer to as "checking in" with your spouse. What we're talking about is an uninterrupted, take-this-really-seriously time to find out what's going on in your spouse's inner life. It can occur over a cup of coffee or meal together (assuming the setting allows for undistracted focus on each other and the conversation), on a long walk,* during a drive, or in virtually any setting in which husband and wife are willing and able to *listen* attentively to one another. In addition to a planned time (for example, every Saturday afternoon for coffee), it also can and should occur as a spontaneous "I need to talk" session.

This is *not* the same as date night, by the way, which has its own valuable place in a marriage. Date night should be a specific activity that ideally involves three mutually enjoyable Rs: recreation, relaxation, and romance—and perhaps a little S as well. Checking in actually *can* occur on a date night if the conditions are right—for example, over a leisurely dinner. A ball game, bowling alley, or karaoke lounge would-n't exactly be ideal venues for this function.

As with any significant discussion, timing can be important. For example, one or both spouses may not feel up for a checking-in session at the end of a long and stressful day. On the other hand, if you've been synchronized in this routine for a while, the opportunity to ventilate and decompress with an attentive and supportive spouse may be just what the doctor ordered when you've "had it up to here" with the kids or the job. If one person wants to initiate a session and the other doesn't feel up for it, a rain check should be accepted, as long as a time is set in the near future for this conversation.

How often should a check-in session occur? If you've been keeping up with each other, you may be able to slide by with one of these sessions every couple of weeks, but we recommend that checking in occur at

---

* If you're one of those type-A, gotta-be-productive personalities, the multitask-ing involved in exercising while you have these conversations should appeal to you.

least weekly. If you've gone for months or years and are just starting to reconnect, you may need to set aside a *lot* of time to catch up on the places the other person's thoughts and emotions have taken him or her. When counseling couples in crisis, Teri will often assign them to do this every night for a prolonged period.

Couples who set aside time for a weekly catch-up session are taking a critical step toward ensuring a long, fruitful, and loving relationship. The flip side of that statement is this: By the time a couple begins marriage counseling, their main source of contention usually is *not* a well-defined issue. Indeed, they might not even be able to identify what their original disagreements were about. Instead, most of their distress arises from the years of anger and bitterness from not being heard.

Every married couple Teri counsels receives a handout titled "Checking In with Your Spouse." It contains some basic ground rules and questions for discussion. You'll find this famous handout at the end of the chapter, at no extra charge. We sincerely hope you'll take the time to ask each other these questions on a regular basis from now on.

Checking in is only part of the solution

You may think, *So all we need to do is check in every so often?* It would be nice if we could truthfully claim that engaging in one particular activity would guarantee an enduring, stable, and satisfying marriage. Yes, regular times for checking in with your spouse should appear on your calendar, for all of the reasons we've set forth. But they are only part of a tapestry of daily decisions that can build—or dismantle—a state of true intimacy for a married couple.

Exercise: Checking in with your spouse

Here are some basic ground rules for this exercise: *Listen* to the other person without giving any negative feedback, advice, or problem-solving solutions, unless your spouse specifically asks for it. One person may ask his or her partner all the questions before switching. If one person ends up talking the whole time you have allotted, don't worry; start with the other person the next time. (Don't let one person dominate the time each week; allow the quieter partner time to organize and share his or her thoughts at a leisurely pace, even if there are pauses during which the more talkative partner is dying to jump in.) Or let each person answer one question at a time. If you have only a short time in a given session, focus on questions 6 and 7.

1. What was the best thing that happened to you this week?
2. What was the worst thing?
3. How did I best meet your needs this week?
4. How did I least meet your needs this week? (Be careful: Don't become defensive when you hear the answer. Just listen!)
5. What could I have done differently in that situation that would have been more helpful for us?
6. What are you the most worried about right now? (*Note:* This is the single most important question you can ask during this session.)
7. Is there any way I can help you with that concern?
8. What are you feeling right now?

3

Communication: Laying Down Weapons of Marital Mass Destruction

Ultimately the bond of all companionship, whether in marriage or in friendship, is conversation.

—Oscar Wilde, 19th-century playwright and novelist,

"De Profundis"

The deepest satisfaction and delights of intimacy, of knowing and being known in marriage, begin and end with communication. So does the process of keeping up with the changes that are unfolding in your spouse's mind and heart. So do misunderstandings, put-downs, red-hot arguments, verbal and physical abuse, and icy silence. Needless to say, communication involves much more than the specific words we humans utter in a conversation. Inflection (sometimes of just one word), tone of voice, facial expression, posture, and touch all speak volumes. Oh, and we didn't mention a critical communication skill that all too often goes AWOL in a relationship: listening. If a spouse feels as if he or she isn't heard, things don't go well. Consider the story of Bill and Janice:

> Within a few years after walking down the aisle, Bill and Janice had developed a well-worn pattern for handling the inevitable irritations that occur in a marriage. Their approach wasn't particularly pretty. Not wanting to sound like a noodge, she would try to overlook little annoyances—his leaving dirty dishes all over the house, for example—until her overall level of dissatisfaction reached a critical mass. Suddenly she would blow up over some seemingly trivial issue. Bewildered by the vehemence and apparent illogic of her outburst, Bill would initially try to placate her by fixing the particular problem. When that didn't seem to cool her anger, he became impatient and would talk over her until she felt steamrolled by his barrage of words.
>
> Because Janice often didn't know herself what was prompting her emotional eruption, she was helpless to articulate it to Bill. The more determined he became to "finish" an argument, the more confused she became. When she was finally backed into the corner by his verbal swordsmanship, she would become mute, leaving Bill confused and angry. Days of chilly, businesslike conversations—the bare minimum needed to run the household— would follow, and then they would gradually drift back toward some sense of normalcy, but without ever resolving, let alone understanding, what had happened the previous week. Every cycle of this dismal dance left them feeling further and further apart.

Does any of this story sound familiar? Do the changes in your life and the issues in your marriage lead to heart-to-heart conversations, arms-length negotiations, or launching of verbal missiles?

Getting a grasp on basic communication is key to recognizing change in your spouse. To keep things simple, we can think of daily communications in marriage as falling into three basic categories:

1. Doing the dailies. These are the conversations about the everyday business of life: "I'll be getting a few groceries; do you need me to pick up the dry cleaning too?" "Can you drive Megan to soccer practice?" "Has last month's bank statement arrived yet?"

2. Dealing with issues. An issue is any topic about which husband and wife may disagree. The potential impact of the topic may be trivial (which way the toilet paper hangs) or monumental (whether or not to have children).

3. Knowing and being known. These are conversations that build intimacy and forge the most powerful bonds between two people. These "close marital encounters of the third kind" are the lifeblood of your marriage—and often everything seems to conspire against your having them. (Remember: They are also the satisfying conversations that happen during courtship, when two people are most likely to be endlessly curious about the inner workings of the other's soul.)

Communication basics

In the last chapter we talked about the importance of regular checking-in conversations with your spouse as a strategy for having those critical "close encounters." But even if you're diligent at setting up the time and place for these, you may not find that you immediately go to soul-to-soul depth every time you sit down together. One major obstacle may be the way you talk to each other during the other 98 percent of your week. Based on Teri's experience in couples counseling and our observations of many married couples over the past few decades, we have two important observations about this subject.

First, you can coexist with someone for decades without experiencing much (or any) intimacy. You may know couples—in fact, you may be one of them—who appear to run a very smooth and even successful home, much like business partners, without having any conversations that tap into thoughts or feelings about their lives.

We should be quick to point out that much can be said for having this type of cooperative and functional relationship between husband and wife. It can provide a stable and peaceful environment for children as they grow and eventually launch into their own adult lives. It can allow husband and wife to pursue worthwhile goals at work and in the community. It can provide ongoing support and even leadership for a church. And it definitely beats the alternative: chaos, disorder, and end-less combat. But eventually it may begin to feel arid—especially when some greener grass comes into view.

Second, every marriage has a few ongoing themes that generate most of the disagreements between husband and wife. No two people entering a marriage are exactly alike. (This is a good thing, by the way. As the old saying goes, if two people agree on absolutely everything, one of them is unnecessary.) When you first become attracted to someone, you are passionately drawn to, and endlessly fascinated by, the other person's "differentness." In the beginning, the other person's unique attitudes and unfamiliar approach to life can be intoxicating. In the euphoric glow of first infatuation, whatever makes your beloved different from you is affirmed without reservation ("You *complete* me, my love!"). But after the honeymoon is over and you settle into to the routines of daily living, the quirks that once seemed so adorable often morph into an increasingly irritating collection of same old same olds.

The differentness between husband and wife arises from literally everything that makes them unique individuals—biology (gender and genetics), personality, intelligence, people skills, how one was raised as a child, how the family of origin worked, education, life experiences, beliefs about the way the world operates, spiritual commitments, you name it. All of these factors drive behaviors that can either engage or frustrate another person, and their unique combination in a marriage sets up several *ongoing themes*—some that forge deep bonds of affection, and others that generate recurring tensions. Depending on the couple's communication skills, emotional stability, family role models, and a few dozen other factors, the tensions can provoke deep conversations, World War III, or anything in between. Sadly, most couples don't recognize, let alone discuss or resolve, their unique ongoing themes—especially in the heat of an argument.

Here are some *common ongoing themes* that can generate conflict within a marriage. Note that one or more of these are likely to emerge as the winds of change blow within a marriage, and that *your communication skills will play a vital role in your ability to manage those inevitable changes.*

Money management. One person feels pleasure, even validation, when buying things. The other derives peace of mind from having a lot of money in savings. One wants to keep track of every nickel the family spends, while the other doesn't know what a check register is. As we mentioned earlier, it's indeed true that couples fight frequently about money. To complicate matters, arguments involving the bankroll usually reflect even deeper ongoing themes.

Security and safety. One person may be more driven than the other to control risks to life, health, and possessions. This may play out in arguments over how much insurance to acquire, where to live, what kind of car to buy, whether to install a security system in the house, when to have medical checkups, what travel destinations are safe, and so on. In our marriage, for example, Paul has always been more compulsive about making sure every door and window in the house is locked when it's time to turn in. He's also more likely to think about having enough insurance for every contingency. (Several times we've nearly come to blows on a trip when Paul has wanted to add all of the optional insurance coverage to the car rental fee.)

Order versus clutter. One person may be much more relaxed than the other about how much stuff comes home to roost, and where. A related issue: One person may hoard like a pack rat, while the other becomes ecstatic when ordering a Dumpster for the weekend. In our marriage, Paul is the one who is likely to say, "I might need that left-handed widget case someday," as Teri gleefully heaves it into the trash.

Whose family was healthier? If one person's upbringing resembled *Father Knows Best* * and the other lived in utter chaos, the person with

---

* *Father Knows Best* has come to epitomize the clichéd Eisenhower-era middle-class suburban fantasy family. Paul recently stumbled onto a rerun that depicted an age-old theme—appropriate boundaries for a daughter and her boyfriend on a date—with surprising finesse (allowing of course for a half-century's difference in cultural norms). Robert Young's character, Jim Anderson, actually came across as a wise, thoughtful, and confident father, unlike the bumbling, incompetent dads who inhabit most sitcoms today.

the (seemingly) healthier family may come into the marriage with the assumption that his or her sense of the right way of doing things should carry more weight.

Who is smarter? This may seem like a weird subject for an ongoing theme, but many marriages begin with an unspoken assumption that one person possesses more intellect or sophistication than the other. (This may occur, for example, when a very young woman marries a much older man, or if one person holds an advanced degree, while the other barely finished high school.) The couple may function—for a while—with the assumption that the viewpoint of the smarter person should prevail when they disagree. That assumption will eventually wear thin as the years pass and the "less smart" person has learned a few things in the School of Life.

Managing ongoing issues

Keep in mind that all kinds of specific issues can arise from a particular theme, and that a particular issue may have multiple themes that fuel it. For example, an argument over sending a child to summer camp could be driven by themes of saving versus spending (if the camp is expensive), safety versus risk (if one parent is worried about the potential dangers of outdoor activities), and differing family traditions (if one parent had rich experiences at summer camp and the other hated it).

In a best-case scenario, here's how issues (of any magnitude) would be managed:

Check-ins are established. Husband and wife have spent a lot of time talking and listening during the first year or two of marriage, during which they've uncovered a number of the ongoing themes that have emerged in their marriage. They also have a basic understanding of the way these themes play out in everyday life, including some of the tensions they can generate.

They've developed a good set of communication skills to talk about issues, big and small, as they arise. Specifically, they've learned how to explain what they're feeling without attacking—or being attacked by—the other person. In other words, they know how to have a good clean fight.

They have enough margin in their lives. They have time not just to talk through disagreements but also to *excavate* them to uncover how they arise from their ongoing themes. (The topic of *margin* is explored more in chapter 4.)

Ongoing themes, whether identified early or later in the marriage, are explored respectfully and peacefully. Feelings about them are aired. Compromises are negotiated. Understanding and appreciation for the other person deepens.

But guess what *actually* happens? Here's how most married couples deal with a disagreement:

An issue shows up. The couple has an argument over the issue. Their clash follows a well-worn track driven by personalities and previous patterns of arguing. More time and energy are spent attacking each other than actually exploring the issue.

The argument comes to an end. This may involve one person caving in to the other, a door slamming, a retreat to a locked bathroom, icy silence, or perhaps, "Can't we talk about this some other time?" When all is said and done, the conflict hasn't been settled in a way that is mutually agreeable or satisfying.

Silence and disconnection follow for some period of time. After several hours, days, or weeks, the withdrawal becomes too painful or impractical to maintain. The couple begins to reengage, usually over daily business that needs to be conducted ("Can you take Austin to school this morning?"). The couple repeats this pattern year in and year out, in all kinds of different scenarios. This recurring cycle of unresolved issues can spill over into the dailies, so that even the most mundane activities of life may become battlegrounds.

Over time the wounds that husband and wife inflict on each other— and not the actual topics of the arguments themselves—become the primary issue in the marriage. The ongoing themes that underlie their fights are never addressed, or even identified, as the marital trench war continues, often for years.

How do you have a good clean fight?

To be a little more delicate, we could say, *How do you resolve an issue in a manner that is both civilized and productive?* Most couples don't know how to have a good clean fight because they don't have a basic communication skill set. Pardon us if you've heard this, but despite the abundance of books and messages about how to "fight fair" in marriage, too many couples talk to each other like Neanderthals, slugging it out with verbal clubs and spears whenever a disagreement rears its ugly little head. While listening to married couples fight like dockside brawlers in the counseling room, Teri has often wished she could put on a striped shirt, blow a whistle, and start calling personal fouls. (We can only shudder to imagine what goes on when there's no referee to call time-out!) Since even hockey players have to abide by some rules of conduct, it's only proper that men and women who have made commitments to love, honor, and cherish one another should do likewise.

Your spouse deserves to be treated with the same basic respect you would offer a co-worker or a total stranger. Teri has heard these lame refrains far too often: "Home is supposed to be the one place where I can just be myself." "Isn't love supposed to be unconditional? Why can't I just say what I think?" If you're more courteous to the bank teller than the person who shares your bed, something definitely needs to change.* (If you regularly insult or explode at anyone who happens to rub you the wrong way, you definitely need work on your fundamental attitudes, or perhaps some anger-management classes.) These communication principles may help as well:

Following are six basic principles that will advance the cause of peace in your home. If these seem elementary to you, you can skip over them . . . provided that you can raise your right hand and, without fear of being struck by lightning, and solemnly swear you're actually following them consistently in your marriage. The other 99.9 percent of you should read on.

1. Use "I" statements instead of "you" statements, and describe how you feel about the issue rather than informing the other person what he or she is doing wrong. Your objective, in other words, is to attack the issue rather than the other person. For example, instead of saying, "You spend every

---

* For a little reality check, the next time you see flashing lights in your rearview mirror, try conducting yourself with the police officer the way you did during your most recent argument with your spouse. If the conversation eventually involves handcuffs, you might need some work in this area.

night sitting in front of the TV instead of talking to me," you're likely to get more mileage by saying, "I really miss having conversations with you. Could we sit and talk for a while without the TV on?"

2. *Avoid questions that begin with the word* why. While you're at it, try to steer clear of the words *always* and *never*. Questions such as "Why do you always drive so fast?" or "How come you never take me out to dinner anymore?" can only be answered in one of two ways: with "I guess I'm just a complete idiot" or with a spirited defense in which the person on the receiving end of the question is determined to prove that he or she is *not* a complete idiot.

3. *Pick the right time and place to discuss an issue.* Not right before you get into bed, or when you're exhausted, or when the baby is crying, the dog is barking, the TV is blaring, and/or the phone is ringing. Pick a time when you're both rested, and a setting where you can be undistracted. You may have to get out of the house, even if simply retreating to the back porch, grabbing a table at the nearest Starbucks, or walking around the block a few times.

4. *It's okay to take a rain check on discussing an issue, provided that you make a genuine and realistic commitment to have the conversation in the near future. No delay tactics!* For example, "I'm really tired right now. Could we discuss this tomorrow morning over a cup of coffee? I'll buy . . ."

5. *Each person should have a chance to state his or her position without being subjected to interruptions, eye rolling, or editorial comments from the other spouse.* One useful and helpful approach is the almighty pen (or whatever item you prefer—a feather, a tennis ball, or any other object that can't inflict bodily harm). The person holding the pen talks,

and the other person must listen. We'd suggest an upper limit of 10 minutes to ensure that the conversation stays focused (and the other person actually stays awake). You'll want to work on one or two topics in one of these exchanges, not determine the fate of Western civilization. The other person may have the almighty pen (and thus speak his or her piece) *only* after repeating back what the first person has said *to that person's satisfaction.* In other words, the first person must feel that his or her viewpoint and feelings have been heard and acknowledged.

It's important to remember that listening attentively to the other person does *not* necessarily imply agreement but rather indicates respect and a willingness to understand what has been said before responding. When the first person is finished, then the other person can take a turn. This might feel like an awkward gimmick at first, but it can be remarkably effective at keeping hurtful verbal salvos from flying back and forth.

6. The need for "do overs" will be inevitable. Like most skills in life— particularly those that don't come naturally—your noble intentions about using all of these civilized techniques to tackle an issue are likely to fly out the window when the moment of truth arrives. This can happen even among the most experienced fair fighters, but it's more likely to occur when you have some entrenched patterns of arguing, *especially* if the issue has some emotion attached to it. It may not be until the second, third, or umpteenth go-around on a topic that you'll be calm enough to exchange your views using these rules of civilized engagement. What matters most is your willingness to keep coming back until the rules of a fair fight are consistently followed.

From "winning" to collaborating

All of these fair-fight techniques are useful, but remember that they are ultimately only a means to an end. *Intentionally transitioning from an adversarial to a collaborative posture while finding the solution to an issue.* This is a very important strategy Teri employs in the counseling room on a regular basis. In the heat of the moment, most people are far more invested in being right and winning a fight than actually resolving their differences. But the reality is that during a dialogue about any issue, large or small, each of you is either opening or shutting the relational door by the way you choose to communicate. If the goal truly is successful resolution, each person's responses and approaches must always have the objective of keeping the door open—even if only a small crack.

Here's an example: Rob and Ellen came to Teri's office seeking help with a dispute regarding their 16-year-old daughter, who was (to put it delicately) acting out. While Rob had always been more relaxed in rule setting with their children, Ellen had been the "enforcer." Though they began their marriage with only modest differences in their approaches to child rearing, they had drifted further apart in parenting styles as each compensated for the other's perceived deficiency.

Teri helped them understand what had happened by drawing a diagram that delineated their differences. Early in the marriage, Rob and Ellen probably could have placed themselves like this on the continuum of easygoing versus strict parenting:

Rob   Ellen

ridiculously lenient ———— *healthy middle ground* ———— *ridiculously rigid*

But over the years, without a communication mechanism in place for finding respectful, compromised solutions to their differences in this arena, they each began reacting to the other's "wrong approach." Each also needlessly (and fruitlessly) moved away from a healthy middle ground:

◄——————— Rob   Ellen ———————►
ridiculously lenient——— *healthy middle ground* ——— *ridiculously rigid*

This drift toward the extremes had one predictable consequence: There was no mutually agreeable game plan for setting the 16-year-old's boundaries. Even more serious was the steady accumulation of hurt feelings between Rob and Ellen as their unresolved disagreement simmered and then boiled over into some serious arguments. By the time they came for counseling, each could detail a long trail of evidence that his or her opinions had been thoroughly discounted by the other.

After Teri drew the continuum diagram, Rob and Ellen were able to understand how each had pushed the other to a more extreme position on the subject of setting boundaries for their teenager. When Rob seemed to dismiss Ellen's opinion that it was best for their daughter to have stricter guidelines, Ellen became more entrenched in her position. In an effort to compensate for her "wrong" thinking about this issue, Rob had become in fact *more* lenient than he normally would have been. Feeling very unsupported, Ellen then became *more* rigid over time in a misguided attempt to balance the scale.

So here was the resulting mess: We now had a 16-year-old who had become a world-class expert at calculating how to play one parent against the other. We also had the more disastrous scenario of two people who began their marriage vowing to watch each other's backs, but who were instead squaring off like boxers in a ring with no referee, both feeling hurt and marginalized by the other.

Over time Rob and Ellen were able to accept the fact that each of them held an opinion on this issue that wasn't "right" or "wrong" but rather was driven by their personalities and what they had experienced in their own families. They realized that they had been derailed unnecessarily because they hadn't recognized these factors, and that working to repair the years of hurt feelings was as important as their need to agree on appropriate boundaries for their daughter. Indeed, after finally hearing each other's hearts and minds, finding an appropriate compromise became a relatively easy task. Once they understood what had caused them to move apart from each other on this issue, they were able to return to their original positions—which weren't really that far apart in the first place.

Rob and Ellen's story illustrates three public service announcements we'd like to make about settling your disagreements:

Public service announcement no. 1. When discussing an issue, the most important goal is to make certain your spouse understands that you're giving his or her viewpoint a careful hearing and that you consider it to be equal in value to yours. Why? Because taking the other person's feelings and opinions seriously demonstrates that you take him or her seriously—and your mate in turn feels respected. You can take communications classes till the cows come home, but if you truly believe that your idea is the only "right" approach and that you don't have to listen to your spouse, the relationship is in serious jeopardy.

Also, even if you do appear to listen but repeatedly outtalk, outargue, outmaneuver, and generally wear down your partner until he or she concedes to your position, you may wake up one day to find that you've succeeded in "winning," but at the cost of driving your mate right out of the marriage.

Public service announcement no. 2. It's important to distinguish your opinions from core values you consider "a hill to die on." Your opinion is just that—only an opinion. And guess what? The vast majority of marital wounds are inflicted in fights over two basically valid, though different, approaches to an issue. Rarely is there a single perfect approach to any of life's challenges, but rather, solutions lie on a continuum that can have unhealthy extremes and yet a lot of room in the middle for reasonable but differing positions.

Obviously, there are situations in which a conflict centers on a core value for one or both people. Whether to do your own income taxes or let H&R Block do them for you is a matter of opinion. Whether to cheat on your taxes involves important moral principles. But even when one person feels that it would be inappropriate, immoral, or dangerous to concede to the other's position, a line can be drawn in the sand—without kicking sand in the other person's face.

Public service announcement no. 3. The more fully heard, understood, and respected you feel, the less important it becomes to get your own way. Trust happens when you believe the other person is always going to act in a way that is most beneficial to you and to the marriage. If you're convinced that your spouse values your well-being as much as (or more than) his or hers, you don't always have to be in high-vigilance mode to protect your own best interests. Compromise is easier when you don't feel that the other person is marginalizing your feelings and opinions—but when you feel unheard and discounted, your heels will instinctively dig in.

Exercise 1: What are our ongoing themes of discord?

Set a time to consider what you think are four or five *ongoing themes of discord* in your marriage. (We introduced this topic on page 46 and provided some examples on pages 47–49.) If you're going through this book with your spouse, each of you should do this exercise privately. Write down your thoughts and then compare notes. Caution: Although the themes you identify may be a source of some current friction, this exercise isn't meant to provoke a showdown. Nor should either of you seize on the themes you've identified as an opportunity to hurl blame and shame on the other. Think of it as a time to explore and excavate in a cooperative mode and hopefully understand the source of some of your everyday issues.

Hint: Don't try this at the end of a long, grueling day or right after you've just tackled the bills. A Saturday morning over a fresh pot of coffee with the kids at a sleepover is a better setting.

Exercise 2: How clean are our fights?

Assign a grade (A, B, C, D, or F) to yourself—and your spouse—on the six basic principles for a good clean fight, listed on pages 52–54. (As with the first exercise, pick an appropriate time to do this—preferably when you're not already embroiled in an argument.) For any themes in which either of you scores a C or less, pick *one* that you're not doing well and make a pact to practice that principle until it becomes more or less automatic. Then move on to another.

4

Some Important Stuff That Affects How You (and Your Marriage) Change

> What counts in making a happy marriage is not so much how compatible you are, but how you deal with incompatibility.
>
> —Psychologist George Levinger

> Each divorce is the death of a small civilization.
>
> —author Pat Conroy, "Death of a Marriage"

We could write a book about all of the factors that come into play when life brings changes to a married couple. Not surprisingly, these factors also play a vital role in the overall health of a marriage—indeed, Teri deals with them every day in the counseling office. While *unexpected* changes in life (or in either partner) often bring conflict to a marriage, *intentional* changes on the part of husband and wife lead to a more intimate and resilient union. We'll be dealing with both types of change in this chapter, though you can readily guess which of the two we would prefer to see more often.

We're going to introduce these subjects by posing nine key questions and then offering a *Reader's Digest* version of our thoughts about them. Obviously we'd like you to think about these questions in the context of *your* life and marriage. Some of these questions primarily impact how you as an individual change or respond to your spouse's changes. (Teri frequently must explain to couples at the outset of counseling that individual stuff will need to be addressed as part of, or before, the actual work on the marriage.) Others mainly affect the how the marriage itself functions as a "civilization," a concept that will begin our discussion.

Key question no. 1

How well have you established your marital civilization? Whether you marry at 20 or 40, you come from a *civilization*—usually the family in which you were raised—where you observed and learned a million and one ideas about how life is lived. These customs and beliefs cover a wide gamut of everyday concerns and responsibilities, from how you hang the toilet paper to the way you celebrate Christmas, and everything in between. Whether the topic is trivial or titanic, we often take our mental checklist titled "The Way Things Were Done in My Family When I Was Growing Up" and slap on a new label that says "The Way Things *Should* Be Done in Our Marriage."

You may not see yourself as strongly attached to or impacted by the family civilization in which you grew up. In fact, you may have noisily objected to the way things were done in your family, especially during your teen years. But even those who seem to jettison the manners and customs of their family of origin (or a bad first marriage) often find themselves unconsciously duplicating the very civilization from which they thought they were disengaged. Why? Because it's *familiar*, and our default setting is to gravitate toward that which is known. There are always exceptions, of course, but we humans tend to find comfort in the familiar and fulfill the old adage that we are creatures of habit. And what has become habit for us has a way of subtly but persistently evolving into what we assume to be the "right" way to do things.

Enter your new spouse. That person comes to the marriage with an entirely different set of the right way to do things. Here's a news flash that you need to keep front and center in your brain: *You cannot assume the marriage will run the way it did in the civilization from which you came. Instead, you need to construct an entirely new civilization.* (This is where *intentional change* is good and necessary.)

Think of it as the United States of _____ and _____ (insert your names). You may have had—and may still have—the strongest bonds of love and loyalty to your family of origin, but when you marry you must understand that you are now the citizen of a new country, a new civilization. This new entity should have its own unique charter, constitution, bylaws, rules and regs, and manners and customs that define the way *you*, this one-of-a-kind married couple, do things. The more clearly defined this entity becomes, the better equipped it will be to deal with the stuff of life and cope with change, whether good or bad, major or minuscule.

How do you accomplish the daunting task of constructing a brand-new civilization? You need to build it brick by brick during hundreds of conversations (hopefully utilizing good communication skills) in order to figure out how your two civilizations will be melded into a unique new entity. Inevitably you'll need to arrive at a number of compromises, and some of these will be a lot easier than others. Agreeing that the toilet paper should unspool toward the throne rather than the wall shouldn't be too hard, but what about your plans for Thanksgiving dinner? If you're still struggling with these issues, bring them up at your next checking-in session, and use the questions at the end of chapter 2.

Key question no. 2

Do you recognize the sovereignty of both you and your spouse? While we firmly believe in the necessity of melding two existing civilizations into one brand-new entity, we are *not* saying that one's personal identity and development should be forfeited at the wedding altar. Nothing could be further from the truth. In fact, it's crucial that husband and wife each understand the autonomy of the other in this new regime. Each willingly submits to the concept of the greater good in carefully collaborating with the other person, but this deliberate sacrifice of one's rights can be healthy only if the other's individuality and boundaries are carefully respected.

A successful marriage resembles two countries that share a geographical boundary and understand the necessity of careful ongoing dialogue and respectful protocols. Can you imagine what would happen if two superpowers came to the negotiating table without a formal system for addressing grievances? What would happen if they hurled insults and threats as emotions flared, never agreeing to listen carefully to the other's point of view and refusing to compromise on any point?

Job no. 1 for newlyweds:
creating a new civilization

When Teri talks with married-couples-to-be, she not only drives home the importance of establishing a new civilization, but also urges them to follow this practical directive: *The schedule of the first year (or more) of a marriage should be diligently protected in order for those civilization-building conversations to take place.* The long and luxurious philosophical discussions that (hopefully) occurred during courtship are both wonderful and necessary for laying the foundation of your new civilization, but they're a far cry from negotiating how the routines of daily life will actually be conducted.

If you're reading this book as a newlywed or a spouse-to-be, you should be keenly aware that it is absolutely critical to keep your calendar as empty as possible during the first year of marriage. Don't volunteer for any new activities (and consider suspending some ongoing ones). Try to avoid getting pregnant.* Don't get a dog. Don't make many social engagements. Keep your living arrangements simple. Unplug your TV. Don't let some needy friend or relative move in with you or even be a guest for more than a few days. Don't go out of town to be with the folks for the holidays. Parents and other family members need to hear a loving, respectful but clear message that you intend to form your own traditions, and that you aren't just an extension of either original family.

---

* Don't get us wrong here: Children are a wondrous blessing, and we absolutely abhor the idea of ending any pregnancy, no matter when it occurs. But if you can delay your first pregnancy for a year, you'll be less distracted as you create your new civilization.

These two countries would quickly find themselves in the midst of a catastrophic war. Sadly, this metaphor describes many marriages. But wars can be avoided, and healthy changes brought about, if each person respects the other's "country of origin" and individual sovereignty when issues need to be resolved.

Key question no. 3

Are you ready to go "all in"? Whether you're marrying for the first time or remarrying and blending two (or more) families, a couple who is in the process of establishing a new civilization will encounter a formidable number of adjustments, negotiations, arrangements, and rearrangements. These are likely to be accompanied at some point by stresses, setbacks, or even outright upheavals, and all of these changes can present obstacles to the process of knowing and being known by your mate. (The stress of building a new civilization is so high in remarriages that we've included a special appendix called "Change in the Blended Family.")

Life's struggles can create formidable relationship barriers, but there's a greater obstacle to attaining a deep level of intimacy. This particular roadblock we call "not being willing to go *all in*." In a poker game a decisive moment occurs when one or more players declare "I'm all in" as they push all of their chips into the pot, betting everything on a hand they believe to be strong enough to prevail in such a gamble. If a couple wants to know and be known by one another in the deepest sense, each person in the new marriage needs to go *all in,* to commit to building a unique, number-one priority relationship. This is essentially the admonition most young couples hear during their first time at the altar, involving "leaving and cleaving": "For this reason a man will leave his father and mother and be united to his wife, and they will become one flesh," reads the familiar passage from Genesis.[1]

For the young newlyweds, going all in will frequently require revising familiar and emotional ties with parents and other family members—especially if one or both spouses haven't spent a lot of time living as independent adults. Those who marry after many years of living as single adults will have some additional layers to negotiate as they form their new civilization, because they bring to the marriage not only the manners and customs of the families in which each was raised, but also all of the patterns they have established while living on their own. Each will have to make room for the other in hundreds of ways and may be reluctant to give up some entrenched habits. This task can to some degree be lightened by mature attitudes that hopefully have accrued over years of independent living.

Key question no. 4

How well do you understand family-of-origin dynamics? All of us have predictable (and usually unconscious) reactions to various situations in life. Although some of these responses arise from basic personality traits that are genetically hardwired, most are formed during childhood in what counselors refer to as our *family of origin.* When changes occur in our lives, and especially when we encounter conflict, many, if not most, of our knee-jerk responses can be linked to the way we were raised, the role(s) we played, and what was modeled in the family—or families—in which we grew up.

Remember what we said earlier in this chapter: We tend to cling to whatever is familiar, even if a rational examination would lead us to the conclusion that some of our favorite "familiars" aren't particularly healthy. If we repeatedly react in certain ways that are counterproductive, understanding the family of origin can provide important insights. This in turn shifts things away from a shame-based response ("I'm/you're such a jerk!") and also lays a foundation for strategies to make positive intentional changes (as opposed to saying over and over, "Oh well, this is just how I am—take me or leave me"). We cannot stress enough how important it is for husband and wife to identify and graciously understand these factors.

Some family-of-origin issues that can impact your marriage in general, and your responses to changes in particular, include the following:

Birth order. Parents being parents and kids being kids, it's possible to predict how your birth-order position—that is, whether you were born first, last, middle, an only child, or one in a pack—will affect your role in the family and, in turn, your behavior later in life. If you have a particular interest in this topic, we would highly recommend Dr. Kevin Leman's informative and entertaining book *The Birth Order Book: Why You Are the Way You Are* (Grand Rapids: Revell, 2004).

Parenting styles. How did your parents demonstrate love for you? How often did you hear "I love you" or "I'm proud of you" from each parent? How did your parents set and enforce limits? Was discipline fair and consistent? Did your parents seem to form a unified mighty fortress in their decisions regarding boundaries and consequences, or did you know that you could divide and conquer if you really wanted to get your way?

Who held the power? What was each parent's role in the family? Did your parents have a hierarchical relationship (where the father was the authority over all) or more of an egalitarian relationship (where Mom and Dad held equal power)? Who *in fact* wielded the power in your family? (*Hint:* It may not always have been obvious.)

Dynamics of family communication. Were you ever encouraged by either parent to identify and articulate your feelings, or were you sent the message that it was wrong to have feelings (or that you shouldn't feel what you *did* feel)? What was it like when your parents disagreed? Was it loud or deadly quiet? How were you affected during and after their heated arguments?

Socioeconomic status. Where was your family on the socioeconomic ladder? Did you feel you had less than or more than your friends? If you were lower on the ladder, were you keenly aware of it growing up, or were you surprised to learn it as you emerged into adulthood? More important, how did your experiences compare with those of your spouse? Have any differences in socioeconomic status between your two families generated some conflict?

Work and play. Was the primary purpose of work to accumulate wealth or to secure resources to supply your family—including spending time together—and to bless others as well? Did either parent believe that play was part of a balanced life, or was the work ethic held in such high esteem that time off constituted laziness?

Holiday celebrations. What were holidays and birthdays like in your family? Do you look back on your childhood Thanksgivings, Christmases, and birthdays with sweet nostalgia or with a shrug of the shoulders? Have you had arguments with your spouse about how, where, and with whom holidays should be spent? Do you try to re-create a Norman Rockwell painting of the traditional family yuletide in your home? If so, are your hopes ever realized, or are they dashed every year?

Spiritual background. If one or both parents held strong spiritual commitments, do you remember these as a positive or negative influence in your family? At any time during your childhood, did you buy in to the religious system in which you were raised? Or did you opt out at some point, and if so, why?

Sex. Were Mom and Dad physically affectionate? Did either parent explain the facts of life to you at any point during your childhood or adolescence? If so, was it a relaxed conversation or a fidgety birds-and-bees lecture during which everyone in the room desperately wanted to be somewhere else? Was sex presented in a negative or positive light? What messages did you get from each parent about sex?

Basic values. What fundamental values were held in highest esteem in your family? Here we're not just asking about what your parents and other family members *told* you, but what was actually *modeled* in everyday life. Most of the values we learned from our parents were taught not with words but by watching how they actually lived.

Alcoholism, addictions, and mental illness. Did you have an immediate member of the family who was addicted to alcohol or drugs? Did one or more family members struggle with anxiety, depression, or more serious mental disturbances, such as schizophrenia? If you were raised in a home where behavioral dysfunctions were like proverbial elephants parked (but not acknowledged) in every room, are you fully aware of their impact on your own emotional growth?

Abuse. Did you experience physical, sexual, or emotional abuse from one or both parents, an older sibling, or another family member? A *yes* answer to this question is such a serious issue that addressing it will require some concerted effort, probably including guidance from an experienced counselor. Those who have survived childhood abuse but have never confronted their history will have great difficulty fully accepting the invitation for intimacy extended by a spouse. (More on this in chapter 5.)

If you've ever had some sessions with a professional counselor, many of these questions should sound familiar. The purpose of understanding how your family of origin affected you *isn't* to wallow in self-pity or blame. It isn't meant to promote a sense of victimization if you had a rotten childhood or smug feelings if your parents did a good job. Most of us grew up in a multicolored (and multilayered) mosaic of pleasant and painful events. And, like it or not, what happens in childhood doesn't stay in childhood. It carries forward into adulthood, marriage, and parenting, and understanding its reach for both partners in a marriage is a critical step in dealing productively with the inevitable changes that will come in your lives.

Key question no. 5

Do you need to establish boundaries in your life and marriage? In 1992 clinical psychologists Henry Cloud and John Townsend published *Boundaries: When to Say Yes, When to Say No to Take Control of Your Life.* The book was well received (and rightly so) and launched a series that includes *Boundaries in Marriage, Boundaries in Dating,* and *Boundaries with Kids.** We would recommend any and all of these.

---

* We would like to propose two additional titles: *Boundaries with Cats* (which would consist of one blank page) and *Boundaries with HMOs* (a five-volume set).

In relationships, boundaries are a way of understanding what you and the other person are, or are not, responsible for. Boundaries can vary enormously depending on the nature of the relationship, and they often change with time. All kinds of problems can develop when the boundaries in a relationship aren't clearly understood, mutually agreed upon, or respected by one or both persons. A good example is the relationship between an employer and an employee, which should be defined by a written job description. If the boss asks a subordinate to pick up her dry cleaning and it's not in the job description, she has inappropriately crossed a boundary. If the employee overheard that the boss is in a tight spot because of an unexpected death in the family, she might choose to volunteer for this errand, which would constitute a voluntary but temporary shift in a boundary.

One might assume at first glance that there would be no boundaries whatsoever within a marriage, where two become "one flesh," but that isn't at all the case. In fact, there are many ways in which boundary problems can affect a marriage. Many of these involve outside forces impinging on the marriage, but some other major-league boundary issues can develop within the marital relationship itself. If not recognized, discussed, and managed properly, they can drive a wedge the size of Texas between husband and wife. Here are three important examples:

1. Parents and in-laws. This classic source of marital conflict frequently arises from misunderstood boundaries. There are countless ways that (usually) well-intentioned parents and in-laws become embroiled in their married kids' lives, but some common areas include the following:

- How the wedding will be conducted

- Where the newlyweds will live and how their house will be furnished
- Where and how vacations and holidays will be spent
- How the grandchildren will be reared

Furthermore, because of housing costs and other financial pressures, it isn't unusual for married couples and their kids to move in with one or the other set of parents, a setup for conflict even under the best of circumstances. Avoiding boundary issues between generations can be boiled down to accepting a few basic responsibilities:

- Married couples need to create their own unique civilization, whether or not they are encouraged to do so by other family members.
- Parents need to remember that their primary purpose over their 20 or so years of child and adolescent rearing is to work themselves out of a job—to prepare their kids for adult independence and responsibilities and then treat them accordingly when the time arrives.
- Even the most enthusiastic grandparents need to remember a word of wisdom once offered by a longstanding friend of ours (who is a seasoned grandpa): "The grandparents' job is to keep their wallets open and their mouths shut." Advice may be given—when requested. It should otherwise be withheld, unless of course a child's life and health are in immediate danger.

2. Excessively prolonged involvement with kids. This is the flip side of parent and in-law issues. A marriage can be derailed when one or both parents stay embroiled in their kids' issues far too long. As we just mentioned, responsibilities should be constantly shifting as children get older. Parents who are worried sick about their kids' misadventures may continue enabling, bailing out, and otherwise perpetuating bad decision making by preventing consequences from playing out in their young lives. This is not only destructive to the adult child but is often detrimental to the parents' marriage as well, because Mom and Dad are likely to disagree about their level of involvement.

3. *Feeling responsible for someone else's mood or self-concept.* This can be a huge boundary problem in a marriage, *especially* when the person with a turbulent mood or black hole of neediness is your spouse. The problem can also arise when the other person is a parent, child, relative, or close friend.

Boundary issues like those we've just described can and will sneak into any marriage, *especially* when they involve people we care deeply about. We'd highly recommend adding to your personal library the original *Boundaries,* and if possible the companion volumes dealing with marriage and kids. A good use of some of your checking-in sessions (remember chapter 2?) would be to read (or listen to, if you prefer the book-on-CD option) one or more of these as a couple, and then discuss how they relate to your own marriage.

Key question no. 6

Are you building and maintaining hedges of protection around your marriage? In 1989, before his Left Behind series became a runaway best seller, author Jerry Jenkins wrote *Hedges: Loving Your Marriage Enough to Protect It.* The book has been revised and republished (Crossway, 2005) and continues to find new readers. This is a good thing. It details both a mind-set and many practical steps that, if implemented, go a long way toward protecting marriages from affairs.

The particular scenario that *Hedges* targets is one we've seen all too often, especially among those who would consider themselves invulnerable to an affair. In fact, we described it in chapter 2. Here's the short version: A married person finds an attentive, nonjudgmental ear with whom to explore thoughts and feelings. The ear is attached to someone of the opposite sex. Conversations ensue and then deepen. More time is spent. Ideas and emotions that should be shared with the spouse are repeatedly diverted to the other person, with whom one doesn't need to worry about the dailies. Attraction grows. Touching occurs. Clothes are removed. At least one marriage sustains a severe, possibly mortal wound. Here's a news flash: *The wound was inflicted long before the clothes came off.*

There are many levels of defense against this scenario. The most obvious is maintaining an ongoing level of intimacy and communication within your marriage that eliminates the need for an emotional connection outside of it. But there are practical measures as well, and these involve deliberately avoiding scenarios in which any type of fuse might be lit—or even *appear* to be lit. We could summarize the principle using a portion of a single verse from the New Testament: "Among you there must not be even a *hint* of sexual immorality."[2] Here's our own amplified version:

> If whatever you are contemplating could remotely be interpreted
> as inappropriate, or might raise the slightest question of impropri-
> ety, or would require an explanation to your spouse, or could set

you up for trouble if the other person turned out to be a wacko, even if your every thought and intention are perfectly innocent and honorable, *don't do it.*

Our shining example for this admonition is Billy Graham. He had a multidecade career speaking to millions of people in every corner of the world. When he started his career, he was literally catapulted to rock-star status. He drew huge crowds.* He was on the cover of national magazines. He met with presidents of the United States and leaders of foreign governments. He was handsome. He was electrifying. He was *hot.* And yet over a career spanning well over 50 years in the public eye, he was never the subject of a scandal, sexual or otherwise.

Beyond his personal integrity and accountability to his leadership team, this achievement involved a practical decision: He would scrupulously avoid any situation—sharing a meal, riding in a car, even entering an elevator—that would result in his being alone, even for a few minutes, with a woman who was not his mother, his wife, or his daughter. Such attention to propriety might seem legalistic or even fanatical in this day and age, but in fact, it greatly simplifies the preservation of integrity and reputation. Nothing can happen when there is no opportunity for something to happen. Life tends to be much more straightforward when you have nothing to explain, spin, defend, or hide. Our

---

* On March 30, 2008, a crowd of 115,300 jammed the Los Angeles Memorial Coliseum for an exhibition game marking the 50th anniversary of the arrival of the Dodgers from Brooklyn. It was the largest audience ever for a baseball game (of course, the Dodgers lost), but not the largest single gathering in the Coliseum's long history. That event occurred in 1963, when 134,254 people came to hear Billy Graham.

advice: Make a commitment to do likewise. (*Hedges* will give you plenty of food for thought, as well as practical suggestions.)

Key question no. 7

Do you need to build margin into your life and marriage? Here's the problem in a nutshell: Some of us have a tendency to say yes to too many requests for our time, attention, expertise, and resources. Our calendars can become a dense checkerboard of commitments involving extended family, friends, work, church, and volunteer organizations. When they're old enough, our kids may grow schedules that make their parents look like slackers. None of these things are bad in themselves. But put them all together, and they create what psychologist and author Dr. James Dobson has referred to as "routine panic"—a perpetual state of hurry, fatigue, and frustration.

A marginless lifestyle can impact your physical, emotional, and spiritual health, as well as the quality of your relationships—especially your marriage. If you think about the themes of this book—dealing with changes in your lives, knowing and being known by your mate, listening attentively, having those undistracted conversations that allow each of you to keep current with each other's thoughts and feelings—you'll be able to figure out in a heartbeat that these goals will be extremely difficult to carry out when you're going one hundred miles per hour every day of the week. At best you may stay congenial as you run your household, but only at a surface level. At worst one or both of you will become increasingly frayed and dissatisfied, and the other will be too swamped to notice.

We won't attempt to set forth all of the excellent principles for creating margin in your life. We will, however, offer our own observations on this process:

Think carefully about the root causes of your marginless lifestyle. You may need some help with this because you may not be aware of the forces driving it. We have some questions for you to consider at the end of this chapter.

Financial pressure by itself can drive a marginless lifestyle. To paraphrase a quip we heard somewhere, are you struggling because you bought stuff you didn't really want and couldn't really afford so that you could impress people you don't really like who really don't care? You know who you are, and you know that this problem is sucking the life out of your marriage. Remember that all of your stuff will eventually become landfill. Read chapter 6; then make a budget, make some hard decisions, give each other some grace, and allow yourselves time to make incremental, *sustainable* changes.

Accept the reality that creating margin in your life won't happen overnight and will involve some pain. The process is a lot like getting out of financial debt. You need to honor whatever commitments you've made rather than abruptly defaulting on them with a resounding but sudden "I quit!"

Avoid adding new commitments to your life unless you subject them to some penetrating questions:

1. *How does this activity fit with the core goals and objectives of your life?* (This means that you and your spouse need to figure out what these are—if you can carve out the time.)

2. *Is this something only you can do?* Here's a big reality check: Only you can think your thoughts, pray your prayers, decide

what you'll eat, exercise your body, be the wife to your husband or the husband to your wife, and be the father or mother to your children. Every other role you might play in the grand scheme of things is replaceable.

3. *Does this pass the end-of-life test?* This may sound morbid, but it's important. When you're on your deathbed, what will you really care about—taking another look at your diplomas, résumé, and portfolio or being with the people you most love?*

4. *If you're going to add an activity to a full schedule, what other activity are you going to phase out to make room for it?* We hate to add another observation from Captain Obvious, but you don't get any minutes added to your day just because you said yes to something worthy.

Consider finding an informal "review board" to help you recover margin in your life. When someone beckons with a new activity, assignment, or other worthy cause, the immediate answer should be, "Let me get back to you on that." Then allow your spouse and a couple of trusted, loving but hard-nosed friends to grill you mercilessly before you add something to your load and schedule. You should require a unanimous and enthusiastic thumbs-up from these people before you press forward.

Remember that margin problems typically involve a lot of commitments to worthy causes. This means that you may feel guilty withdrawing from some of them. Acknowledging our limits is actually healthy for us. It helps remind us that God *can* run the universe without us, and

---

* A reality-based version of an infamous bumper sticker slogan would read, "He who dies with the most toys . . . dies."

that other people can take care of things when we can't. A wise friend once gave us the following challenge: You have to divide your commitments into three categories—good, better, and best. Then you have to get rid of "good" and "better."

In 1994 we first heard Richard Swenson, a family physician, author, and eloquent speaker, introduce the concept of *margin* as the space between our load and our limits. Swenson's book *Margin: Restoring Emotional, Physical, Financial, and Time Reserves to Overloaded Lives* (Colorado Springs: NavPress, 2004) describes the problem in fascinating and painful detail. If you need further help, we recommend this book.

Key question no. 8

Do you or your spouse need to address self-concept issues? For decades a small army of authors and motivational speakers have told us about the harmful fallout from low self-esteem, and its importance has been elevated almost to the status of a religious creed. We actually have some issues with the assumption that acquiring self-esteem is the cornerstone of life and health.

For now, we would like to focus on a more straightforward notion: a *healthy self-concept*, which has important implications for marriage. Too many people enter marriage with enormous unmet needs and look to their partner to "complete" them. This (usually unspoken) expectation can suffocate a spouse who was hoping for a partner in marriage, not a restoration project. And even if you enter the marriage with a sturdy identity, how you see yourself will definitely change in response to the events and seasons of your life.

Self-concept means, simply, how you see yourself. When we refer to a healthy self-concept, we're describing someone who sees himself or herself realistically and who thinks and functions in such a way as to live a satisfying and productive life. Needless to say, there are many dimensions to one's self-concept, but for the moment we'll concentrate on the arena of human relationships, where a healthy self-concept includes the following components:

1. *A reality-based assessment of personal strengths and weaknesses.* There is no false humility or inflated sense of capabilities.

2. *A basic acceptance of personal responsibility.* The person with a healthy self-concept has a realistic "internal locus of control"— a basic belief that he or she has the power to impact what happens to him or her in life.

3. *The ability to self-regulate one's emotional landscape.* Although humans crave (and thrive on) interpersonal relationships, the capacity to maintain a steady mood and outlook in the midst of aloneness is the mark of one who isn't dependent on others to "inform" her about how she should view the world.

4. *The ability to accept and retain a "steady state" belief about authentic expressions of affection from other people, even during their absences.* The analogy Teri most often uses to explain this concept to clients is a picture of the heart as a container. When a person with a healthy self-concept experiences emotional intimacy with a spouse, friend, or relative, the warm feelings generated during that encounter are "deposited" in a solid container. When he or she is away from the other

person, he or she continues to trust the expressions of intimacy; they remain in the heart even during the other person's absence, and the memories of affection can be trusted.

5. *The belief that one's own feelings and opinions can be trusted.* The person with a healthy self-concept is willing to put his or her thoughts on the table during a discussion because he or she believes they are valid enough to be heard. If someone disagrees, he or she can listen and consider the other viewpoint without feeling shamed, humiliated, or defensive.

6. *The freedom to enjoy the journey.* Many who are in the limelight and/or strive to hold power in this world are driven by an assumption (which may or may not be consciously acknowledged) that more money, more fame, more degrees, more awards, and more recognition will lead to a feeling of "finally good enough." The person with a healthy self-concept understands that the grand prize in life is the journey itself, the people who accompany you, and ultimately the Creator of both your life and journey on this planet— and afterward.

7. *The ability to wholly trust another person.* (More on this to come.)

8. *The capacity to be others-directed.* For the person with a healthy self-concept, the question of worth has already been answered, and emotional energy that used to be employed in a desperate search for approval can now be diverted to really seeing, hearing, and valuing others.

Note to husbands (but wives listen in, since this applies to some of you): You may see yourself as cool and calm, and not one of the angst-ridden wimps who wear their hearts on their sleeves (and everyone else's). Here's a big news flash: *Emotions are happening in your soul on a regular basis and are impacting you—and those around you—whether you recognize them or not.* You may feel like the captain of your ship, with a firm grip on the helm, but under the water emotions are regularly pushing the rudder and changing the pitch of the propeller. They drive not only your opinions but all kinds of behaviors and reactions as well, including physiological responses that often send people to their doctors' offices or the nearest emergency room.

Paul has spent hundreds of office visits evaluating headaches, tight muscles, pounding pulses, shortness of breath, cramping intestines, fatigue, and a host of other complaints that were ultimately found to be physical responses to stress and other emotions. "But, Doc, I don't *feel* upset about anything" is the bewildered response to this diagnosis. Aah, but that's the point. Whether or not they are identified, named, or understood, emotional currents flow and impact not only you but also your spouse, your kids, your co-workers, and anyone else who crosses your path.

So how does all of this self-concept and feelings stuff affect my marriage? We've used the phrase "knowing and being known" repeatedly throughout this book because we passionately believe it's the foundation for intimacy. The kind of knowing we're talking about doesn't involve gathering a database of facts about someone. It's a kind of knowing that happens only when you *experience* someone else completely. It's not the knowing that occurs during courtship when you put forth only your very best self, counting on the other person to see this idealized version through a generous filter. It's a knowledge that comes only when two people commit to a sustained effort to know themselves and each other, warts and all. Sadly, *this effort isn't likely to be successful when either the husband or the wife is desperately seeking self-worth.*

Simply stated, the person who arrives at the wedding altar without a healthy self-concept is bringing a lot of need into the marriage, possibly more than any single human can realistically meet. When the honeymoon is over and the spouse is no longer able or willing to deliver a continuous stream of affirmation, the needy person becomes panic-stricken because she is so dependent on her marriage partner to help her feel good about herself. In a real sense, she is looking to her spouse to supply what her parents didn't (or couldn't) give her.

Her bottomless pit of need can eventually evolve into a steady stream of demands, as her energies become focused on "making" her bewildered (and increasingly resentful) husband supply her with non-stop approval. On a broader scale, the self-preoccupation that always accompanies an obsessive concern over worthiness makes it difficult to accomplish the tasks necessary to build a strong marriage: truly hearing the other person, not feeling threatened when faced with the necessity for compromise, marshalling internal resources when one's partner has had a setback and is "down for the count," maintaining a perspective that allows one to assess the other person's need, and so forth. It's a paradox that in order to be a really good partner in a relationship that is formed for the purpose of establishing exquisite intimacy, one must first have the ability to stand alone!

An important note: In the preceding paragraphs we identify the person with the unhealthy self-concept and more overt neediness as the wife. In Teri's experience this tends to be the more common scenario, especially in marriages where the wife stays home while the husband has the opportunity to be affirmed in the workplace. However, there are plenty of men with this problem as well.

What if you've read the characteristics of a healthy and unhealthy self-concept and realize that one or both of you seem to fall on the unhealthy side of the ledger? This is an important and emotional subject, and if at all possible, you should seek some help from a trained counselor and/or pastor as you begin to explore it. You might be resistant to the process of excavating its roots. You may want to avoid dredging up painful memories from the past. You may be uncomfortable with the idea that the reason you have an unhealthy self-concept is because of the way you were treated by one or both parents. A fierce loyalty to Mom and Dad—often driven by an unmet need for approval—may interfere with this process. Or you may be concerned that exploring how your parents treated you could conflict with a commitment to honor your father and mother. However, it's important to note that you can address whatever they may have done poorly without being condemning or disrespectful.

Figuring out what happened in the past, of course, is only part of the process. You'll need to address how your unmet needs are playing out in your marriage and in your parenting (if you have kids) and then develop some different patterns of thinking and behaving. This won't happen overnight. In fact, count on it being a journey, more like a cross-country walk or even a marathon rather than a sprint. As we'll discuss momentarily, there are also some important spiritual dimensions to this issue that should definitely be explored.

What if it's dawning on you (or you've realized for some time) that your spouse has this problem? Perhaps it has taken years for you to figure out that your spouse has wanted you to play the role of the perfect, unconditionally loving parent, and that you didn't sign on for that assignment. You may be tired of dealing with defensiveness, demands, and communication that isn't straightforward. You may find that your prevailing mood is anger, your energy has been sucked dry, and your desire is to withdraw.

You have an important task before you that may tax every ounce of your resources and patience. A major challenge that may require some time on your own in the counseling room is figuring out which issues both of you need to address together, and which need to be addressed individually. Otherwise, you can become worn out trying to fix what is truly out of reach, or you may be tempted to put everything wrong in your marriage on your spouse's side of the ledger.

Once you have a reality-based sense of what's going on and how it might have come about, there will come a time to approach your spouse about working on these issues. Unless a counselor advises otherwise, this should be framed as an invitation—"I think we can work together to make things better"—rather than a do-or-die demand. If your spouse's answer is an ongoing no, you'll still have some important work to do. You'll need to understand what you can and cannot be responsible for in this relationship. As we discussed in the segment on boundaries, *you cannot assume total responsibility for your spouse's mood and self-concept*, and you don't have the luxury of assuming false guilt whenever these head south for the winter (or any other season).

What is your self-worth actually based on? (And why does it matter?)

We mentioned at the beginning of the previous section that we had some issues with the notion that pumping up one's self-esteem is the ultimate secret to a happy life. But isn't that the same thing as having a healthy self-concept? Not exactly. Our concern is that focusing exclusively on self-esteem fails to address a number of critical issues of the human condition—including some that affect marriage. So what can go wrong if the pursuit of self-esteem is the be-all and end-all of life? Plenty.

First, there's the unsettling possibility that a person can have a generous amount of self-esteem and apply it toward a successful career as a drug dealer, assassin, slave trader, sexual predator, dictator, or cult leader. What are we likely to call someone whose self-esteem fills the room? Egotistical. One might counter that egotists and evildoers who appear very confident are actually overcompensating for low self-esteem or childhood wounds. This may be true in some cases, but certainly not all. Either way, self-esteem alone doesn't hold up as the moral compass and ultimate reference point for our lives.

Second, let's assume that we're decent folks who are doing our best to pursue our goals, bolster ourselves with positive self-talk, and make copious plans for self-improvement. We may feel pumped up about our potential, our affirmations about impending

(continued)

success, our formulas for dynamic living, and so on, especially after reading a book, listening to a motivational speaker, or attending a weekend seminar. *Rah-rah-rah! I'm really wonderful on the inside; I just have to realize it and unleash it.* But in the middle of the night, when these activities can no longer keep our minds occupied, some unsettling trains of thought may pull into the station. We remember our shortfalls, our bad habits, our addictions, our actions that served our interests at someone else's expense. What lives in the darkest corners of our hearts—what we've done, what we've thought, what we've pursued on the Internet—crawls out to mock our aspirations. We're repeatedly forced to face a primal fear: "Maybe I'm *not* good enough . . ." In his own dark night of the soul, *Saturday Night Live*'s self-help enthusiast Stuart Smalley moaned, "I'm going to die homeless, penniless, and twenty-five pounds overweight."[3]

Third, even if we're not ruminating about less-than-stellar behavior in the middle of the night, we may be plagued by another nagging sense that our existence simply has no meaning. Does my life really have any significance at all? This is especially likely for those who have bought into the notion that, to quote astronomer Carl Sagan in the first line of his book *Cosmos*, "The cosmos is all there is or was or ever will be." It's painful indeed to go anywhere near the black hole of insignificance, where one's existence simply doesn't matter to the universe. We'll employ myriad strategies—frenetic activity, relentless achievement, mood- and mind-altering drugs, pursuit of power, serial relationships—to avoid the despair of that bleak place.

Consider an alternative to the relentless pursuit of self-esteem that establishes the basis of our worth, unflinchingly addresses our failings, and settles the question of our place in the universe. Set forth in the pages of the Old and New Testaments, this worldview involves knowing and being known by the Creator of "all there is, all there ever was, and all there ever will be"— including each of us. For a moment we need to walk a fine line between stating the obvious (for those who are well acquainted with the biblical account of the human condition) and assuming too much (for those who may not be familiar with the account and may be getting jumpy: *Oh no, Martha, they're gonna spring a sermon on us . . .*). But what we're about to set forth here has a direct bearing on the whole premise of this book, so bear with us.

If you aren't familiar with the overall arc and details of the Bible's worldview, here's the short version: God exists, He created the universe, He loves each of us, and—amazingly—He actually wants each of us to have an intimate, loving relationship with Him. (If you take a moment to think about the size of the universe and the number of people who have ever lived on this planet, this is a mind-boggling idea. *How can God keep close tabs on billions of people on this planet—and, while He's at it, many more billions of galaxies?* It's beyond our finite brains to

(continued)

comprehend, but we have it on good authority.) An authentic relationship requires freedom to choose whether to accept love that is offered and to offer love in return, and God has in fact given that freedom to each of us. Unfortunately, the default setting of the human race has been (and still is) to opt out of a relationship with Him. The results are readily apparent in every daily newspaper—war, crime, deceit, abuse, hatred—as well as in less spectacular but no less painful manifestations we've all experienced in one way or another—lying, cheating, addiction, disloyalty, injustice, envy, love of stuff more than love of people, and so on.

The restoration of this relationship is the subject of the entire Bible and comes to a climax in the birth, life, teaching, miracles, death, and resurrection of Jesus. Through Him it is now possible to enter into a relationship with God—but the process may not sound much like a recitation of self-esteem affirmations. The key word is *repent*—a word that has some baggage attached to it from preachers on street corners with bullhorns, but actually carries a wealth of meaning. As one writer* put it,

> Turn around. Give up. Wave the white flag. Abandon the idea that you're in charge, the master of your fate. . . . Stop justifying your ego, your betrayals, your gossip, your harsh words, your lust, your bitterness. Stop making excuses. Stop trying to prove that you're not so bad after all. Stop denying what you know in your gut when you can't sleep at three in the morning. Turn toward home. Let your Father embrace you. Accept

the pardon. Take the gift of forgiveness and life that was so costly—the one that only Jesus, and not you, could pay for. Thank Him for enduring what you deserved. Thank Him for rescuing you. Put Him in charge of your future. Let Him have your relationships, your job, your stuff, your time. Give Him access to the breadth and depth of your mind and emotions. Give Him permission to haul out the junk, to make repairs, to restore, to redecorate.

This is the most important step you will ever take, and no one can do it for you. Others may have tried to pressure you to do so in the past, but God will not. The door is open, with warmth and light on the other side, and it's up to you to decide to walk through it. . . . This is literally like saying "I do": one moment you're single and the next you're married, even if it took you months or years to arrive at the altar. Jesus described it as being born a second time. A new life begins, and it never ends, even when the physical body wears out.[4]

This step of repentance ultimately settles the questions that the relentless pursuit for self-esteem can never answer:

What is my worth based on? It's based on nothing I can do, be, achieve, earn, beg, borrow, or steal. It arises entirely from my relationship with the loving Creator of the universe, who knows me inside and out. That means I'm free—to the degree that I can grasp this reality—to relax, stop taking myself so seriously,

(continued)

pay attention to what other people need, and do something about it, without calculating what's in it for me every second of the day.

What about all of the rotten stuff I've done and thought, do and think, and will no doubt do and think in the future? I can fully and honestly acknowledge it for what it is—thoroughly and utterly rotten—without making excuses, blaming someone else, or feeling permanently discouraged about it.

Does my life really have any significance? Consider the words of the psalmist:

> Where can I go from your Spirit?
> Where can I flee from your presence?
> If I go up to the heavens, you are there;
> if I make my bed in the depths, you are there.
> If I rise on the wings of the dawn,
> if I settle on the far side of the sea,
> even there your hand will guide me,
> your right hand will hold me fast.[5]

If the Creator of galaxies, blue whales, DNA, lightning, and sunsets is paying attention to me, the answer would be a resounding yes.

---

* Actually the writer was Paul—one of the authors of this book, not the apostle.

Key question no. 9

Am I knowing and being known by God? A couple of pages ago we mentioned that beginning our relationship with God can be compared to exchanging vows at the wedding altar. It's no accident that the Scriptures contain a number of passages comparing our relationship with God to a marriage, with astonishing implications: This relationship with the Creator of the universe involves intimacy, communication, *knowing and being known*. In his classic book *Knowing God*, J. I. Packer makes the following observations:

> The quality and extent of our knowledge of other people depends more on them than on us. Our knowing them is more directly the result of their allowing us to know them than of our attempting to get to know them. When we meet, our part is to give them our attention and interest, to show them good will and to open up in a friendly way from our side. From that point, however, it is they, not we, who decide whether we are going to know them or not. . . .
>
> What matters supremely, therefore, is not, in the last analysis, the fact that I know God, but the larger fact which underlies it— the fact that *he knows me*. I am graven on the palms of his hands. I am never out of his mind. All my knowledge of him depends on his sustained initiative in knowing me. I know him because he first knew me, and continues to know me.[6]

If you ponder that idea for a while, you can begin to see a number of fascinating similarities: Many of the same types of behaviors that build or impair intimacy in marriage also build or impair our intimacy with God. Indeed, you may have established your relationship with God some time ago—perhaps decades in the past—and now find yourself struggling with a sense that things are dry, flat, perhaps even lifeless on the spiritual front. In assessing the reasons for this state of affairs, several of the themes in this book might be worth considering:

1. *Are you checking in with God on a regular basis?* Is your communication honest, open, candid, and frequent, or is it stilted, repetitious, disingenuous, and rare? In your conversations with God, do you do all the talking? (Here's another way of thinking about this: If you were talking to your spouse the way you talk to God, would he or she be bored stiff?)

2. *Do you try to keep a lot of secrets from God?* Are you confident enough in your relationship that you can be open with Him about the dark corners of your life? We can't help but wonder if God is more heartbroken or amused by our pathetic efforts to hide some of our activities from Him. A moment's reflection brings to mind the two-year-old who tries to "hide" from his dad by covering his own eyes.

3. *Are you more interested in knowing "about" God or knowing God?* There's a world of difference between the two. Just as you can know a lot of information about your spouse without having a clue what he or she is thinking or feeling, you can have the entire Bible memorized without having an experiential sense of God's presence on a day-to-day basis.

4. *Do you carry a lot of baggage from your past (including your family of origin) that affects your relationship with God?* If you say, "Our Father, who art in heaven," does your earthly father come to mind, with all of his attributes (for better or worse)?

5. *Do you ever spend undistracted time with God?* Or are you unable to sit still for more than a few minutes without thinking about the next 14 things you gotta do? Is your schedule so packed that you don't have time to converse in a meaningful way with your spouse or children, whom you can see, let alone God, who is invisible?

Exercise 1: Identifying the basic values in my family of origin

What fundamental values were most often demonstrated in your family while you were growing up—not what you were *told* by your parents as much as what was actually *modeled* in everyday living?

Take as much time as you need to list what you believe were the basic values (for better or worse) that governed your parents' decision making in daily life. (This may take more than one session.) To stimulate your thinking, we've listed below not only several types of values but also some statements that express how people feel about (and thus act on) them. We're usually unaware that we hold these kinds of operating beliefs, and yet they fuel our daily decisions and reactions. Indeed, a primary objective in therapy is helping an individual discover the beliefs that are actually "driving the boat."

The list of values for discussion we've provided is far from a comprehensive inventory. It's intended to start you thinking, so don't limit yourself to just these values. If you're doing this exercise with your spouse, compare your final lists and see if you're surprised by anything.

- Physical health
- Mental health
- Spiritual health and growth
- Family
- Financial security
- Loyalty
- Respect
- Social status
- Generosity
- Intimacy
- Intelligence
- Beauty
- Friendship
- Achievement
- Service
- Adaptability
- Integrity
- Wisdom
- Stability
- Freedom
- Laughter and playfulness

Here are a few examples of statements that express basic values:

- "Taking care of one's health is more important than anything else—what does wealth matter if you're dead?"
- "Image is everything. No matter what goes on behind these closed doors, we must look good on the outside. No one can know about our problems."
- "Generosity toward those less fortunate is more important than accumulation of personal wealth."
- "The children's happiness and welfare comes ahead of the marriage."
- "Rules are for regular people who are too dumb to get around them."

- "Compliance is better accomplished through fear rather than love."
- "What you do when no one is watching should be the same as what you do when someone *is* watching."

As you list the basic values in your family of origin, think about these questions:

1. What on this list has been incorporated into your adult life?
2. What on this list did you consciously reject and replace with an different value?
3. What on this list has unconsciously been brought into your adult life that you would *like* to replace with a different value?
4. Does what you and your spouse actually *do* every day align with what you say are your core values? (*Hint:* Think about where you spend your time—and your money. Your checkbook will reveal a lot about what you truly value.)

Exercise 2: A few tough questions about your boundaries, hedges, and margin

Spend some time journaling your answers to the following questions. If you do this with your spouse, set aside some time to compare your answers.

1. Who is the biggest boundary buster in your life? In what way(s) is that person intruding in your life? What boundaries could you begin to set with this individual? Do you need any help doing this? (*Hint:* Boundary busters aren't always enthusiastic about respecting these types of changes in a relationship.)

2. On a scale of 1 to 10 (with 10 being the highest level of confidence), how "affair proof" do you consider your marriage to be?

3. Where would you consider your marital civilization to be most vulnerable to the subtle intrusion of a third party?

4. Do you feel as though you're laboring to "keep the plates spinning" in various areas of your life (marriage, kids, career, church, friendships, finances, health)? In what area(s) of your life do you spend the most time feeling inadequate (or like an utter failure)? In what area(s) do you feel you're doing well?

If your life is short on margin, think carefully about the following questions:

1. *Are you driven by the need for approval?* Approval addicts have a terrible time saying no to any request from anyone, no matter how unreasonable. (They'll do so eventually, however, but only when they become angry because they can't keep everyone happy.)

2. *Are you trying to define yourself (and, in particular, your worth) with a string of titles or accomplishments?* The beginning of wisdom is the realization that these at best will bring only fleeting satisfaction.

3. *Are you overly optimistic (i.e., unrealistic) about how much time and effort a particular commitment will actually require?* This usually arises from a need to look good in other people's eyes, since the response "I honestly don't think I can do what you're requesting right now" usually makes other people unhappy.

Exercise 3: The foundations of your self-concept

We would encourage you to think carefully about the following questions that focus on your self-concept. Write your answers in a journal, and consider sharing some of these with your spouse during one (or more) of your upcoming checking-in sessions.

1. On a scale of 1 to 10 (10 being the best), how would you rate your self-concept, based on the description given in this chapter?

2. Was your mother's approval conditional? If so, what was it conditioned upon? Did you ever finally win her approval?

3. Was your father's approval conditional? If so, what was it conditioned upon? Did you ever finally win his approval?

4. Were you allowed to express your feelings or opinions as a child or adolescent?

5. Has your self-concept improved or become worse during your adult years? To what do you attribute the increase or decrease?

6. Is there a correlation between your self-concept and how you conceptualize your relationship (or lack thereof) with God?

7. Do you believe that God thinks about you individually? If so, what is the first thing you imagine comes into His mind when He thinks about you?

Endnotes

1. In the King James Version, Genesis 2:24 reads, "Therefore shall a man leave his father and his mother, and shall cleave unto his wife: and they shall be one flesh."

2. Ephesians 5:3, emphasis added.

3. *Stuart Saves His Family*, directed by Harold Ramis (Paramount Pictures, 1995). Stuart Smalley, the character created by comedian (and now U.S. Senator) Al Franken, was famous for the mantra he recited endlessly to himself in a mirror and that ultimately became the title of this tongue-in-cheek self-help book: *I'm Good Enough, I'm Smart Enough, and Doggone It, People Like Me!* (Dell, 1992).

4. Paul C. Reisser, *Complete Guide to Family Health, Nutrition and Fitness* (Carol Stream, IL: Tyndale House, 2006), 399–400.

5. Psalm 139:7–10.

6. J. I. Packer, *Knowing God* (Downers Grove, IL: InterVarsity, 1973), 37, 41.

5

Bedroom Blues

Sex is a conversation carried out by other means. If you get on well out of bed, half the problems of bed are solved.

—Widely attributed to British actor Peter Ustinov

Before we got married, my wife used to say, "You're only interested in one thing." Now I've forgotten what it was.

—*Milton Berle's Private Joke File*

Sex Begins in the Kitchen

—book by psychologist Kevin Leman

As individuals and as a couple, you'll discover that changes will inevitably cross your path in life. More often than not, they'll actually alter that path or even cause you to wonder whether you have a path at all. We've spent a fair amount of time (and pages) describing the foundations that strongly affect whether or not your marriage will thrive. Now we need to roll up our sleeves and look at some of the most common areas of life in which important and predictable changes will occur. (These also happen to be the topics that keep marriage counselors busy.)

So . . . here's the $64 question:* How will your marriage weather these changes? Will it thrive? Will intimacy—the kind we described in chapters 1 and 2—grow, or will it wither? Will your marriage run aground? Will it implode? (If you skipped over these topics to get to this sex chapter, we'd strongly urge you to take a deep breath [or a cold shower], turn back, and read the preceding chapters.)

First, we're going to plunge feet first into the two topics in which marriages are almost certain to experience major changes and that couples fight about most often. We've already mentioned them, but they deserve a formal entrance. Those topics are (drum roll, please): sex and money.

Then we're going to look at a number of predictable changes that occur over the life of a long-term marriage. We're well aware that not all marriages last from young adulthood to an advanced age and that many are reboots at various stages of life. However, the foundations (chapters 1 through 4) apply to all marriages, as does most of what will follow.

With those preflight advisories completed, fasten your seat belts. It's time to talk about sex. We'll start with a look at a typical scenario described to Teri:

---

* The term *$64 question* as a synonym for a tough problem had its origins in a popular radio program called *Take It or Leave It* that ran on CBS through the 1940s, and then on NBC (renamed *The $64 Question*) from 1950–1952. It would inspire the hugely popular TV quiz show *The $64,000 Question* that ran on Tuesday nights from 1955–1958. Restaurant business, movie attendance, and crime rates reportedly dropped dramatically during the show's broadcast time.

Jenni checked her watch. The signals from Randy throughout the day had been unavoidable. It had been more than two weeks since they'd last had sex, and she didn't know how much longer she could issue rain checks. She was exhausted even though the last kid had been wrestled into bed 10 minutes earlier than usual, and Randy had done more than his "fair share" all day.

She was without excuse, and her heart sank. She ran through her mental checklist. There was one project that *had* to get done before bed. She so wanted to have a little "me" time for the first time today. She wondered if she could get by with a quickie tonight. Probably not. Randy had bought her that cute little silk nightie for her birthday . . . three months ago, and the tags were still attached. She sighed. Nope, Randy would be hoping for the full works tonight, and he had really been so attentive to her these past few days. Besides, he was already upstairs . . . waiting. She didn't feel he deserved to be turned down once again. If only she wanted sex as much as he seemed to! She pulled herself up and tried to shake off the vague resentment she felt as she headed for the bedroom.

Randy checked his watch. He was more than ready to indulge in some marital privileges with his wife. It had been more than a month since they last had sex, and then it hadn't been the unhurried, intense sexual interlude he'd hoped for. He was beginning to feel truly rejected as Jenni tossed out one lame excuse after another in response to his hints that some lovemaking would be appreciated.

What happened to the cuddly little sex kitten he fell in love with? He considered himself to be a pretty good husband. He went with her to marriage seminars and read the touchy-feely books. He had cut her a lot of slack during the childbearing and baby-care years of their marriage. But the youngest had been out of diapers for months now. He was still waiting for things to return to normal. He'd gone to more seminars and read more books. They'd attended some marriage retreats. He brought flowers and took out the trash. He'd tried to do all the things he was told would bring back his wife's sex drive.

But nothing seemed to have brought back the sexual appetite for *him* that Jenni once had, and he was beginning to give up hope that it would ever reappear. Where *was* she? He'd knocked himself out being more than attentive this week. In the past few months, he'd started resenting how many "good husband points" it seemed to require to motivate Jenni in this department.

Finally, footsteps. As Randy heard Jenni coming up the stairs, his mood changed from bleak to hopeful.

Ask any marriage and family therapist (including the one who cowrote this book) what married couples fight about most often in the counseling room, and you'll usually hear that the topics involve budgets and bedrooms. Most of us can figure out why money is on this short list: There's usually less of it available than either person would like, and whether money is scarce or abundant, it's rare that any two spending agendas precisely align. (For further details, watch any session of Congress.) But why sex, and what exactly is the source of most of the conflict? If sex is such a wonderful, exciting, and fulfilling activity, how does it become the source of disappointment and pain in a marriage?

You probably have an idea—indeed, our scenario involving Randy and Jenni may have hit a little close to home—so we'll cut to the proverbial chase by unpacking the dynamics of a common scenario.

For most couples, sexual chemistry isn't an issue during courtship. In fact, it usually provides a major *ka-ching* factor in the original attraction. Many unwisely believe that feeling madly in love is reason enough to head for the bedroom long before they even think about marriage, let alone tie the knot. Others, out of respect for God and each other, attempt to restrain themselves from "doing it" before they say "I do." Some of these couples may slip and yield to sexual involvement before they arrive at the altar; others take deliberate steps to stay out of bed while eagerly anticipating that event on their wedding night. Either way, young men and women who are surging with hormones and emotions rarely feel the need to ask how to keep their libido* humming after vows are exchanged. That question seems utterly ridiculous when both are usually thinking of little *else* during that glorious season of a relationship.

Then, sometime after the wedding, it happens—or more specifically, "it" begins to happen less often or stops happening altogether. At some point (usually after the first child is born), the wife's libido goes AWOL, an event that bewilders her and exasperates her husband. She begins to feel guilty for failing to live up to a message poured forth every week in the popular media: "If you're a 'normal' woman, you should look and feel sexier with every passing year!" The man starts

---

* You probably already know this, but the word *libido* is a clinical term for sexual desire. If you're in polite company and need to use a word to describe the condition of having increased sexual desire (or just want to sound highfalutin), you can use the word *libidinous.*

feeling like a dog begging for leftovers. The wife becomes resentful that her husband "seems interested in only one thing." He in turn becomes resentful that she now apparently considers sex—something that makes him feel not only physically satisfied but truly loved—to be at best a duty and at worst an annoying but unavoidable chore.

And here's the most painful thing of all: Because the wife feels guilty for constantly putting off her husband's requests for sex (whether or not delicately put), and because the man misinterprets his spouse's lack of libido as lack of desire for him personally, *neither of them is capable of having authentic communication about this painful issue.* Aside from an occasional angry outburst from either side, there is virtually no real discussion that might provide insight and a chance for corrective measures to be taken. Along with the pain comes a paradox: Despite the fact that films, television shows, talk radio, popular music, books, and magazines (especially those beckoning at the supermarket checkout stand) routinely contain sexually themed material that ranges from candid to explicit, few of us are comfortable discussing our *own* sexuality with anyone, even our spouses!

There are in fact a number of important reasons why marital sex can involve more thorns than beds of roses. Many of these involve basic differences in the wiring between men and women, including physiology, hormones, and emotions. A number of other reasons for the thorns grow out of predictable changes, especially in women, that occur with the passage of time and the seasons of life. These are all relatively straightforward and can be addressed—often with satisfactory results for both husband and wife—with some basic education and conversation.

Some marital sex issues are far more complicated and may require medical evaluations, extensive counseling, a lot of patience, and acceptance of the possibility that they can be *improved* but not necessarily *fixed* to everyone's satisfaction. In this chapter we'll look at the gamut of these issues, starting with one that can set the stage for marital bedroom troubles long before husband and wife even meet.

Toxic cultural messages and the erosion of trust

Beginning in the 1960s, Western societies rapidly abandoned a longstanding cultural consensus that marriage was the appropriate arena for sexual activity. Whether called a "sexual revolution" or the "new morality" (although it wasn't particularly new), this moral free fall disseminated a sexual philosophy that might be summarized as follows:

- Sex is okay in any way and with anyone, as long as there is mutual consent, no one gets pregnant (unless she wants to), and no one gets hurt.

- Transmitting an infection during sex isn't a good idea, so don't leave home without a condom.

- Sex is usual, customary, normal, natural, expected, and inevitable if there is mutual attraction, and in many cases when there isn't. The duration and quality of the relationship, let alone love, commitment, and marriage, need not factor into the decision to have a sexual liaison.

- If you're postponing sex until marriage, you must be physically unattractive, socially inept, psychologically impaired, or a religious fanatic. If you advocate abstaining from sex until marriage, you're imposing your narrow, outdated, unrealistic, and unworkable personal (usually religious) views on others. Get your head out of the nineteenth-century sand!

In our medical and counseling practices, we regularly seek to counter the cultural expectation that casual nonmarital sexual activity is the norm. We're particularly adamant with adolescents, who may not have had the opportunity to hear this viewpoint expressed by a health-care or counseling professional. We could spend pages describing all of the painful fallout from unintended pregnancies and sexually trans-mitted infections, not to mention the moral and spiritual issues that have been thoroughly marginalized by the popular media. But here we want to focus on another consequence of nonmarital sex: beliefs and attitudes that become hardwired in the brain (especially for women) and are problematic for future relationships.

The ability to trust absolutely, which is essential to a healthy mari-tal bond, becomes an increasingly elusive fairy tale with each aban-donment experience that inevitably occurs after a sexual liaison has been broken off. A number of survival skills accrue that enable a per-son to avoid experiencing pain, loss, and a sense of betrayal in the wake of serial couplings and uncouplings. Each encounter erodes emo-tional innocence and sculpts an ever-hardening cynicism that serves as a form of self-protection. Eventually the capacity to feel completely secure with another person withers, and in its place grows a global dis-trust of the opposite sex.

Compare this with the experience of two people who have waited until marriage to initiate their sexual experience. For them the wed-ding night can be a time of discovery and bonding, and whatever they might lack in technique can be learned pleasantly enough at their own pace. Not surprisingly, the landmark 1992 National Health and Social Life Survey (NHSLS) found that those who reported the most physical and emotional satisfaction with sex were the married couples.[1]

Like the blooming of a rose, a healthy sexual response (*especially* in women) is dependent on the right circumstances over a leisurely course of time. Just as a rose is ruined when its petals are forced open prematurely, sexuality can be seriously damaged if it doesn't develop in the context of unhurried exposure to nurturing conditions. For a woman, the ability to enjoy an uninhibited and healthy sexual response requires that her sexual experiences begin in a setting of complete trust, respect, and love. But if her sexual initiation occurs in a nonmarital relationship, it's unlikely that she will experience this nurturing context, even if sex occurs while she is feeling desperately "in love" with someone. All too often, the context is that of an immature, predatory, or even abusive relationship, especially when sexual experiences begin during adolescence and *inevitably* when they occur during childhood.

Men also can be emotionally devastated by the breakup of one or more relationships that involve sexual intimacy. And men who have voluntarily and enthusiastically engaged in sex with numerous partners before deciding to settle down may bring a lot of emotional and physical baggage of their own into a marriage. They may have repeatedly experienced sex with partners who have had a variety of agendas and lovemaking techniques, and they may bring expectations for nonstop sexual novelty and excitement that have been shaped by viewing the shallow groping portrayed in pornography. But truly meaningful sex is built on a stable and more mature relationship in which sex is freely given and accepted by both individuals.

Here's an example of how trust can become a major issue in the bedroom:

Jim and Trisha were married in their 40s, a remarriage for both. Trisha had grown up hearing her mother transmit an unrelenting message that "sex is dirty; men just want one thing" to her four daughters. Forbidden to date during high school, Trisha went off to college ill-prepared to negotiate her way through the world of hormonally charged young men. She fell in love with and married the first guy who treated her well, and they finished college together in married-student housing. Over the next decade, Trisha had two children and her husband had more than that number of affairs. Their marriage ended in a bitter divorce, confirming Mom's oft-repeated opinion that all men are scum-sucking bottom-feeders.

Trisha swore off men forever and embraced the role of a single working mom raising two children. For more than a decade she adamantly refused all attempts by her friends to set her up with various available males. Occasionally she would acquiesce and go on a couple of dates with someone with whom she felt willing to dip her toe in the water. But inevitably these men would pressure her to plunge the rest of her body into the water as well, leaving her feeling both bewildered and unsafe. The world of opposite-sex relationships continued to be foreign territory for Trisha, and she remained truly content with a life focused on her great kids, engrossing work, and loyal girlfriends.

But one day romance struck: Mr. Right appeared, both unbidden and unavoidable, on her landscape. Jim was the coach for her son's baseball team. He was everything her first husband was not—handsome, self-confident, charming, mannerly, great with kids, solidly and profitably employed. His own children had just launched and were out of the picture, except for occasional family get-togethers. Jim conducted an irresistible campaign and succeeded in winning Trisha's heart, and eventually her hand in marriage as well.

Winning her trust in the bedroom was an entirely different story, however, and their struggle with physical intimacy eventually led to their seeking marital therapy.

Over the course of a year, they explored early messages they had heard about sex in their families and elsewhere, their individual assumptions about what should and shouldn't happen in the bedroom, and their mutual feelings of frustration over their sexual misalignment. Because they've both been willing to learn about male and female sexuality, take some specific direction from Teri, and most important, listen to each other, they are well on their way to establishing a safe bedroom in which each person truly trusts the other.

It has taken time for Trisha to allow herself to believe that here, finally, is a man who won't see her merely as a means to sexual gratification, and she has been able to remove much of the emotional armor she would routinely don prior to bedtime. She's working hard to try new things in the bedroom, and he's working equally hard to accept her boundaries, making sure she feels secure in his love, even if their sexual palette is less colorful than he would prefer.

Later in this chapter we'll look at some problems caused by various forms of damaging nonmarital sexual encounters, but it's also important to understand that sexual issues will arise even when a couple becomes "one flesh" under the best of circumstances. In an ideal scenario, both husband and wife have intentionally reserved and preserved their sexual initiation for the wedding night and have enjoyed exploring this dimension of their lives within the security of their marriage bed. What could go wrong?

All too often, men and women—even those who have done the right thing, sexually speaking—are relatively clueless about the sexuality of the opposite sex in general, and their own mate in particular. Men, who usually have a consistent and persistent interest in sex throughout adulthood, are particularly unlikely to understand the changes that their wives are experiencing in this department as the years pass. And so, gentlemen, we'll start by giving you a few important news flashes about the seasons of sexuality that your mate is likely to experience over the years of your marriage.

Big, important news flashes for husbands

Here's the scoop on women and their sex drive: *There are seasons to a woman's libido*, that driving need to engage in sexual intercourse for the sake of a physical release. Generally speaking, a woman experiences a high level of libido when she is in the courtship phase of life and when she wants to make a baby. She may also feel a little frisky during the fertile time of her monthly cycle. Other than that, she is far more likely to experience a sexual *response* than an actual sex *drive*. And much to the consternation of her husband, the ingredients that ignite or extinguish her sexual response on any given day may involve a complex and ever-changing recipe. One of our favorite illustrations of this state of affairs is a photo of the cockpit of a space shuttle, with its vast array of controls and readouts. This, we point out, represents a woman's sexuality. Then comes a photo representing male sexuality: a light switch on a wall, in the "on" position.

As we've said before, married women are usually bewildered and frustrated when they experience an apparent decline—or complete disappearance—of their need for physical passion, especially after a child or two has been added to the family. They're regularly reminded of this situation at the supermarket checkout line, where magazines bedecked with curvaceous goddesses proclaim, "Wild sex after 50—women just can't get enough!" or "Forty new ways to drive your man wild in bed."* As she scans these headlines while loading diapers and dog food onto the conveyor belt at the register, the average married woman responds in one of two ways: (1) disdain—"You've got to be kidding! What planet do these women (with their army of hairdressers, personal shoppers, and nannies) come from? They need to wake up and smell the Windex"; or (2) despair—"I don't look or feel anything like this picture, which apparently is what normal women experience. I'm completely abnormal and defective."

Equally (if not more) frustrated is her husband, who may be

---

* We can never figure out how these magazines are always finding new ways to drive men wild. What didn't they know two months ago when they ran the same headline? Actually, it isn't that difficult for a woman to drive her husband wild: One come-hither look while releasing the first button on the blouse will generally do it.

wandering in a sexual desert, wondering if his wife knowingly put on an act during courtship. For many men, this is the area of life that most fits the title of this book: "When it comes to sex, my wife isn't the woman I took on our honeymoon. What happened?" Men, your wives were *not* playacting during courtship. They were hormonally primed to feel optimal sexual desire.

As we said earlier, women have predictable seasons of physical desire: when they're seeking male attention, when they want a baby, and sometimes during a brief window of opportunity during the fertile time of their monthly cycle. Period. *For the other 95 percent of her adult life, a woman's ability to be a generous sexual partner who enjoys physical intimacy in marriage is heavily dependent on how she is feeling about the entire relationship.*

Why does this happen? Why do women so commonly experience a high level of sexual desire before they marry only to see it shift to a lower gear once they've entered into the security of a committed, till-death-do-us-part relationship? This transition has long been the subject of both male laments and jokes (of variable taste) about postmarital sex, or the lack thereof. There are a host of reasons and contributing factors (and every couple's situation is different), so much so that we could write an entire chapter or even a book on this subject. For the moment, however, we'll offer a bottom line: *This change in a woman's libido is the rule rather than the exception.* It isn't a game or a trick perpetrated on unsuspecting grooms, and accepting it as a reality is the beginning of marital sexual wisdom.

Ten years into her marriage, with a child (or three) underfoot and, not uncommonly, a paycheck to earn as well, is a woman in the same place she was on her honeymoon, sexually speaking? Definitely not. Ten years into his marriage, with ever-expanding responsibilities and vocational kingdoms to conquer, is a man thinking about his beloved night and day? He may be, but more likely he's taking more than a few things for granted.

So let's back up and repeat an important statement: *For the vast majority of her adult life, a woman's ability to be a generous sexual partner who enjoys physical intimacy in marriage is heavily dependent on how she is feeling about the entire relationship.* This means that the single most important thing a husband can do to get more sex is to love his wife the way he did while he was courting her. Over the long haul, a wife is motivated to be sexually generous and responsive when she feels that she is her husband's number-one project in life. And how does she get that message? How does her husband say, "I love thee"* over months, years, and decades of married life? Writers, speakers, songwriters, and greeting-card manufacturers have offered their advice for generations, but we'd like to "count the ways" we consider particularly important.

First and foremost, it's critical to keep up with your wife's thoughts and emotions. In other words, never lose track of the person she is and is becoming. Go back and read chapter 2, and remember that soul-to-soul intimacy fuels physical intimacy, especially for a woman.

Second (and a corollary to the first exhortation), become a perpetual student of your wife's interests and delights. Needless to say, these encompass

---

* "How do I love thee? Let me count the ways . . ." is the beginning line of a famous love poem from Elizabeth Barrett Browning to her poet husband, Robert Browning. For some deliciously old-fashioned fun, try reading this couple's love poems out loud to *your* spouse.

much more than a candlelight dinner and receiving flowers on special occasions, though such gestures don't hurt. In what situations is she happiest? What does she enjoy doing, reading, seeing, and hearing? Where does she like to go? What does she dream of doing? If you know these things, you can make wise decisions about gifts, vacations, date nights, and your overall priorities as a couple and family. In doing so you cause her to feel loved and cared for. If you're clueless or deliberately override her repeatedly in many of these areas, guess how enthusiastic she *isn't* going to be in the bedroom.

Third, honor her with your words. Honor her both in public and behind closed doors. We've already talked about communication and the ground rules for discussing day-to-day issues in chapter 3, but don't underestimate the impact of what you say every day on your wife's sexual generosity. It should go without saying that abusive language, name calling, and insulting comments, whether in private or (worse) in front of others, violate the vows you uttered on your wedding day. Some couples, however, become expert at stealth attacks—subtle nips and jabs and jokes at the other person's expense. One at a time, any of these might seem mildly amusing. With ongoing repetition, they become verbal termites chewing their way through the foundation of a marriage. Here's an example of a husband who learned this the hard way:

Sam was always quick on the verbal draw, a guy who could find a clever quip for any situation. Maggie was gorgeous but a bit scattered and often prone, as the old adage goes, to put her mouth in gear before fully engaging her brain. While they were dating, Sam found her spontaneity engaging—her knockout figure didn't hurt—but it wasn't long after the wedding that he began to take some sly shots at her verbal gaffes and general lack of organization. Friends began to cringe as Maggie became the subject of some of Sam's revamped dumb-blonde jokes, or when he would pointedly correct her in midsentence while she fumbled to recount some recent event.

After a decade or so of rehearsal, Sam could tell enough Maggie stories to create his own sitcom, and he would do so at the drop of a hat to get a satisfying laugh in almost any social setting. When their marriage hit a particularly rough patch at the 15-year mark, he was taken aback by the rage that began to erupt from his wife—and her complete unwillingness to share her bed with him. Only in the counseling room, when she had his full attention, did he come to understand how his cutting remarks—all in good fun, he thought—had seriously wounded their marriage and killed her affection, sexual and otherwise, for him.

We are happy to report that Sam and Maggie recently renewed their vows. Both have done hard work in the counseling room, and Sam has revamped the way he speaks to (and about) his wife. Needless to say, there has been a major thaw in their bedroom.

Fourth, serve her on a day-to-day basis. Kevin Leman's book title *Sex Begins in the Kitchen* says it all, but here are some examples if you need inspiration:

- If she has been chasing toddlers all day and is hitting the wall at 6:00 PM, guess what will cause her to feel loved when you walk through the door? The wrong answer: "Wow, what a mess! Hey, what's for dinner?" The right answer: "How can I pitch in to help?"

- Shoo her out of the kitchen and take care of the dishes.
- Take over the kids' bath- and bedtime routine while she puts her feet up.
- Put gas in her car so that she doesn't have to hassle with the self-serve pump.
- Give her a foot massage.

A few more news flashes for husbands

Why can't I get a little affection? Most of the husbands Teri counsels desire more physical affection from their wives. Why does that well often seem to go dry?

Here's a common dynamic that every husband needs to understand: Consciously or otherwise, a wife withholds physical affection (hugs, pecks, pats) because she knows her husband can physically go from zero to sixty a lot faster than his car. At first he may be looking only for a quick hug—he may be literally heading out the door to work—but it doesn't take much for him to take a fast detour into overdrive: "Hey! Let's have sex right now!" At that particular moment his wife may be (1) not experiencing any sexual desire, (2) already facing a ridiculous schedule for the day, and/or (3) not feeling well loved overall. She doesn't want the zero-to-sexty progression to begin, so she'll avoid the hug in the first place. Her husband feels like a reject: "Hey, all I wanted was a little hug!" Which leaves the wife to smirk: "Oh, *really*. You and I both know what your 'little hugs' lead to!" Which leaves the husband to respond in bewilderment, "And that would be the worst possible thing that could happen between us today? Thanks a lot!"

This problem actually isn't too hard to fix. The simple fact is that a man *can* honestly approach his wife for a simple hug and proceed to a desire for sex within 30 seconds or less. Sorry, this part can't be helped; it's how men are built. If his wife could just respond to the invitation for a hug and then feel free to say, "Not now, Buster," in a good-natured way when she sees him shifting into second gear, things would be much better. This is called flirting, and most married couples lose this playfulness after a few years because the wife feels guilty and the husband is stewing with frustration about this issue. Sex has become a serious source of irritation for both partners. To make matters worse, most couples don't feel comfortable talking honestly about hugs, sex, and what happens in between—a problem we'll revisit shortly.

How about checking the mirror? Can we talk for a moment about your body and grooming? Wives aren't likely to be turned on when their husbands allow themselves to develop a sizable "spare tire," or when they pay attention to clothing, grooming, or bodily aromas only when it's time to go to work. How aroused do you think your wife is going to become when the odor from your armpits could take out a small elephant? And that eternally untucked shirt is going to be "cute" only if your relationship is humming along well and your wife truly finds that look engaging. Hot tip: It's okay to ask her if she likes your choice of clothes, haircut, and facial hair (or lack thereof). You can't stop the aging process, but you can take care of your body and make some ongoing efforts to look presentable to your wife. This is but another way of expressing your love and commitment to her.

What about the big O? Men, are you ready for some sexual stereotypes to be shattered? Guess what? Your manhood, and your wife's love for you, isn't proven by her having an orgasm on a regular basis. Most husbands Teri works with operate on a deeply held belief that "if my wife will have sex with me, that confirms I'm a stud and she loves me. Better yet, if she has an orgasm, her ecstatic response not only confirms my manly prowess but *really* proves that she loves me."

Here are a couple of reality checks: First, a wife can experience a gamut of emotional responses during sex, and passionate excitement may not be her default setting. Very often her sexual encounters are accompanied by feelings of affection for her husband without any expectation that she will become fired up—which, as we will see momentarily, isn't necessarily a bad thing. Second, unlike men, women don't have a physical need for an orgasm. They certainly don't mind when it happens, but it's not the "gold standard" of a successful sexual encounter.

In Teri's counseling experience only a small percentage of women report that they routinely experience orgasm during sex. In fact, she has been surprised at the number of clients over the years who have eventually confessed, shamefully, that they're not even sure what an orgasm *is*.

What the average wife gets from sex most of the time is some combination of the following: (1) knowing that her husband is going to be in a good mood for a while, (2) feeling relieved from the guilt of how long she's already put him off, and (3) knowing she can actually say "no, thank you" for a few days without guilt. On the plus side, she may experience (4) feelings of closeness and, on really good days, (5) actual physical arousal, up to and sometimes including an orgasm. Please note that number 5 isn't exactly the routine experience for the average woman, and often she has no way of predicting when the fuse will ignite and the fireworks will go off. (Yes, yes, we know there are a lot of exceptions to this statement.)

Here's the really big news flash that Teri repeatedly tries to impart to husbands in the counseling room: *If you would change your expectations for your wife's response during a sexual encounter, you'd probably have sex with her more often than you do now.* Why? Because if men could wrap their brains around the fact that short and (hopefully) sweet encounters—we would use the less clinical term *quickies*—are usually just fine with your wife, she'd probably say yes more often! If your wife senses that the earth must move for you to feel loved, this will present a major dilemma. If she's worn out and looking at six hours of sleep plus a full agenda the next day, or if she just can't generate much in the way of a sexual response, she's likely to keep delaying sex "just one more night."

Frankly, it usually takes time for a woman's body to rev up. Or she may be tempted to "put on a show" just to hurry things along. But a five-minute session without the pressure to be orgasmic? Not a big deal. Let's go! You're happy. Your wife is happy because her husband is happy. Everyone is happy. And if sex is happening more often via these brief encounters, she won't be feeling constant guilt about meeting her husband's need for sex. Being "de-guilted" means that she feels free to say no to a request for sex—but it also means that she is more likely to be playful in this arena.

Are we suggesting that married women are never interested in the full-blown romantic interlude, complete with a secluded rendezvous, candles, massages, and slow, luxurious sex? Heavens no! A healthy, realistic sex life for a married couple with children and full agendas is going to be made up of a lot of quickies interspersed with some intentional big productions and a number of encounters somewhere in between those two extremes. Each couple needs to figure out a pattern that is satisfying for both husband and wife—*and this will change over the course of their marriage.*

When the wife has more libido
than her husband

Without fail, whenever we speak to a group about sexual issues in marriage, we're approached by people (usually women) whose marriages don't fit the cultural norm. We've described the typical scenario where the husband is always doing the asking (or begging), and the wife is usually putting him off; however, in a number of marriages the wife's sex drive exceeds that of her husband. At the risk of oversimplifying what may be a complicated issue, we'll describe two basic variations on this theme:

1. *The husband's libido seems to have declined with the passage of time.* In this case, the question to consider is *What changed?* Possibilities include the following:

- *Medical issues,* such as a decline in testosterone levels, medications that affect libido, or chronic illness.

- *Physiological issues,* such as erectile dysfunction, can lead to a reluctance to engage in sex for fear of an embarrassing or demoralizing replay of a previous misfire.

- *Relational issues* for men that raise a barrier to sex are *not* necessarily about conflict in the marriage. This is far more likely to affect wives, who need the emotional temperature of the relationship to be warm to find sex appealing. (As we mentioned earlier, a guy can be interested in sex even if he's just had a blistering argument with his wife. In fact, he can be interested in sex *during* the blistering argument with his wife.) More commonly, a man may lose sexual interest in a spouse whom he no longer finds visually appealing. This is especially common if the relationship has grown cold and/or contentious.

- *Environmental issues* may include fatigue from a demanding work schedule or distractions in the home (especially lack of privacy). Often he'll find that sexual interest and performance will improve during a true time-out, such as on a weekend at a quiet bed-and-breakfast inn.

2. The husband's libido has always been low. The reasons for this may be more complex and may not necessarily reflect the state of the marital relationship itself ("I love my wife, and I'm not unhappy in our marriage; I'm just not that interested in sex"). Often, deep-seated themes may be playing out, including sexual-identity issues or fallout from abuse during childhood. (Sometimes a man has a lower-than-average libido, and there may be no explanation other than the fact the *some* individuals have to be on the low end of the measuring stick in order for there to be an "average.")

For any of these scenarios we strongly recommend counseling, both individual and marital, and in most cases, a medical evaluation as well. To these you'll need to add a considerable degree of patience, since the solution may not be obvious, or may require a lot of effort on the part of one or both partners, or may be evident but unyielding even to diligent work on everyone's part.

Big, important news flashes for wives

If your sex drive has taken up residence on the far side of the moon, it's more distressing to him than you probably realize. For most wives, libido is drastically reduced during the childbearing years. What most wives don't understand is the effect this disappearing act has on their husbands. For wives, the loss of a sex drive is an irritating mystery. For husbands, it's a profound loss that is quietly (or openly) grieved. A powerful bond develops during the intense sexual passion that usually characterizes the early stages of a marital relationship. (Needless to say, if there has been an absence of physical fervor since day one of the marriage, there is an entirely different set of issues that need attention.) Being the object of a young wife's sexual fervor is deeply satisfying on so many levels that a man will remember and replay those experiences in his mind for the rest of his life. Needless to say, he will long for it and mourn its apparent passing.

If a couple has had any kind of coaching or counseling about physical and emotional developments in marriage, a husband may have an intellectual understanding that his wife's diminished sex drive isn't a negative assessment of how she feels about him as a man. But there is an intense grief over the loss of this precious aspect of the early relationship. Because the wife doesn't feel the same level of grief, it's normal to marginalize the husband's sense of loss and to begin believing that he's only slavishly addicted to sex itself.

So another important news flash for wives is this: *Rather than discount something because you don't understand it, we ask that you accept the reality of your husband's feelings about this subject, just as we have asked your husband to accept some things about you that don't necessarily make sense to him.* We do understand that you cannot willfully produce a sex drive, but you *can* take your husband's feelings about this a lot more seriously. While you may not have a volume control for your libido, you *do* have the power to choose to become more intentional about sexual generosity.

Not terribly shocking news flash: *Men are strongly visually oriented.* When the image of an attractive woman—whether in person, on a page, or on a screen—arrives at the male retina and transmits to his brain, there is immediate interest and potential arousal, even when he's strongly committed to sexual morality and loyalty to his spouse. This immediate interest has nothing to do with the woman's identity, intelligence, personality, accomplishments, or moral character. It's literally hardwired into the male brain, and attempts to prevent it from occurring when the female stimulus is present are futile. Quit punishing your husband for having a *ka-ching!* moment when a gorgeous woman walks through his field of vision. He isn't being disrespectful to you just because he has this initial reaction. He *is,* however, being disrespectful if he chooses to linger on the vision for more than three seconds!

A man's libido not only remains active and relatively constant throughout his adult life, but it also typically is ready and willing to initiate sex at a moment's notice. A not-so-old adage says that in sexual matters men tend to be like microwaves—heating up fast and sounding off in a few minutes when they're done—while women are more like Crock-Pots, offering a delicious payoff after some careful preparation and a day of simmering. A couple may have had a difficult week, a long and tiring day, and little communication (or even an ongoing argument) through the evening. For the wife, nothing in the past 72 hours has remotely inspired any interest in sex. But before bedtime her husband sees her walk by in a clingy nightgown, and he's ready for sex *right now*, regardless of what has happened over the past several hours. Unlike most women, men generally don't need a period of feeling loved and cared for before they want to engage in sex. In fact, a man may crave sex even in the midst of conflict or during an emotional dry spell, because he assumes—not necessarily correctly—that if his wife is willing to have sex, it must mean that hostilities are ending.

Believe it or not, men don't "just want sex." Men desire love and connectedness as much as women. Many wives have a difficult time grasping the fact that a husband hears "I love you" when his partner is sexually responsive. A wife may honestly feel that she is saying "I love you" in countless other ways—bearing and mothering his children, for example—and may be perplexed and frustrated that these seem to pale in comparison with the importance of sex on a frequent basis. Because spirited sex is perceived as a declaration of love, a man may feel rejected (or even punished) when his wife displays a lack of enthusiasm in the bedroom and a seemingly endless list of excuses why sex must be put off . . . again.

Sexual generosity. We are fierce advocates for women not participating in sex when they're the object of ongoing disrespect or outright abuse from a spouse who, in so doing, repeatedly violates his wedding vows. On the other hand, we strongly encourage a woman to put a great deal of intentional effort into creating a generous and participatory role in sex *when she can honestly say that her husband is doing his best to reciprocate and respectfully love her in a way that is meaningful to her.*

Wives, you may think that all you have to do is show up once in a while and be the receiver, but every so often it's really important to initiate a sexual rendezvous with your husband. Teri consistently hears from husbands how powerfully they would hear "I love you!" if their wives would just occasionally surprise them with an invitation, direct the encounter, and try something new. (In many ways this sends the same kind of powerful message to a man that an unexpected bouquet of flowers sends to his wife.)

Women, get your flirt back on! Again, we want to stress that we aren't talking about becoming a Stepford wife,* blindly catering to a spouse who has no regard for your needs, opinions, and feelings. Nor are we talking about a wife trying to use her sexuality as a way to placate or manage her husband. With that important caveat stated, you don't have to always wait for him to initiate a positive cycle. Think back to all the ways you happily and naturally instigated playfulness during the dating phase—goofy little notes, playing footsy during a movie, offering to get him a snack, and so on. Remember how much care you put into your appearance when you were trying to impress him?

It's the responsibility of the husband to love, honor, and cherish his wife, regardless of the impact that years of living, childbearing, and other forms of wear and tear have had on her physical appearance. Period. It doesn't hurt, however, when wives do what they can to make themselves more physically attractive. It's one of many expressions of love for the other person, and one of many responses to feeling

---

* Based on the 1972 novel by Ira Levin *(The Stepford Wives)* and two film adaptations, the label "Stepford wife" refers to a woman who plays a role of cheerful, mindless, and robotic submission to her husband's every whim.

respected and cared for. If you care about your home, you spend time and energy on its upkeep. You do this because you want to create a place that's inviting and pleasant, where relationships grow and memories are made. We would urge you to make the same effort concerning your body and physical appearance. We think you'll be pleasantly surprised at the return on your investment. (For more ideas, author and radio counselor Dr. Laura Schlessinger has addressed the subject of "get your marital flirt on"—and treating your husband with all-around respect—in her book *The Proper Care and Feeding of Husbands*. [HarperCollins, 2003].)

Learning how things work

Many otherwise well-educated adults are surprisingly ignorant about the anatomy and physiology of their own and their spouse's reproductive systems, even if they've had a number of sexual experiences before marriage. Unfortunately, what they *have* learned may be a piecemeal mixture of facts and misinformation gleaned from a variety of sources of variable reliability: a sweaty-palmed birds-and-bees lecture from Mom and Dad years ago; the lowdown from an older sibling, an "experienced" friend, or a health-education class; or perhaps some steamy scenes in movies, romance novels, or even pornography. But a reality- and morality-based understanding of how things work (or don't work) in your body is a necessary part of greater intimacy in the bedroom.

There are some good books on basic sexual anatomy and functioning that provide some fundamental and straightforward information. If you were raised in a "don't ask, don't touch, be ashamed of your bodily functions" kind of family, you'll probably need to subject yourself to a bit of an educational process. Additionally, women in particular have sometimes been brought up to regard the sexual parts of their bodies as dirty. In such cases, it might be appropriate for this person, in the safety and privacy of the bath- or bedroom, to have the book in one hand and a mirror in the other. (We don't give the same "homework" to husbands because they usually have their bodies thoroughly mapped out by age 11.)

As we mentioned earlier, Teri has talked to a surprising number of otherwise educated, sophisticated women who have confessed, with great embarrassment, that they aren't even sure what an orgasm *is* and therefore aren't sure whether they've ever had one. Many women mistake sexual arousal for an orgasm, but in fact, the latter is as definitive as a male orgasm—there is no doubt when one has occurred. A sizable number of women never experience orgasm, however, and they should feel no shame attached to their uncertainty about it.

Doing the "lab"

The term *sex therapist* often raises unsettling visions of some eccentric, kinky "specialist" directing a couple as they try various techniques under the clinical glare of fluorescent lighting. Although this scenario would be highly unethical in any professional setting, a marriage therapist who is helping a couple work through issues of sexual dissatisfaction *is* likely to give explicit direction for "lab" that is done in the privacy of the couple's bedroom. When starting this type of therapy with a couple, Teri will actually recommend a complete sexual hiatus for a specific period of time. (How long? That will be tailored to the needs of the particular couple, with the average length of time being two to four weeks.)

The purpose of this temporary abstinence is to enable the couple to revisit a time in the relationship when they hadn't yet experienced this degree of physical intimacy. It takes the question "Is this going to end in sex?" off the table and allows the partners a chance to recover emotional intimacy that has been eroded—or perhaps experience it for the first time. Additionally, if one spouse (usually but not always the woman) was a victim of early sexual abuse, it gives that individual time to work through those issues without the usual expectations of sex.

Husbands usually object to this assignment at first ("What? This is going in the opposite direction of what I had in mind!"), but by the time they get to Teri's office, couples usually aren't having much sex anyway, so it doesn't really cost him that much. In fact, even though sex is off-limits during this stage, husbands often report a greater degree of satisfaction because they begin to receive at least some degree of physical affection for a change.

During the period of sexual abstinence, the couple works through a series of exercises called "sensate focus," which allow each person to concentrate on the other physically while reducing anxiety about performance. These exercises, which begin with nonsexual touching, can help a couple identify what (other than orgasm) is mutually enjoyable.

With this background in mind, we now want to turn to three factors that can derail a healthy sexual response in men and women, both as individuals and in a marital relationship: (1) early sexual abuse, (2) being raised with negative messages about sex, and (3) sexual wounds sustained from choices made during adulthood.

Early sexual abuse

Teri is continually amazed at the number of clients who have been victims of early sexual abuse and yet don't recognize it as such, because it didn't involve genital penetration. It's a common experience in the counseling room to ask about early sexual abuse, hear a negative response, and then watch the uncomfortable, dawning recognition rise in the client's features as the following definition of early sexual abuse is read aloud:

> Sexual abuse occurs whenever a person—child or adult—is sexually exploited by an older or more powerful person for the satisfaction of the abuser's needs. The range of abuse is broad; it includes verbal, visual, or physical sexual activity that is engaged in without consent. Sexual abuse is a felony in all fifty states. *Verbal sexual abuse* can include sexual threats, sexual comments about the person's body, lewd or suggestive comments and inappropriate discussions. *Visual sexual abuse* includes exposure to pornography, to any sexually provocative scene, to exhibitionism, or to voyeurism. *Physical sexual abuse* is much broader than intercourse (forced, unforced, or simulated). It includes any touching that is intended to sexually arouse the abuser. It can also include exposure of the victim's body to others.[2]

Early sexual abuse can set off a chain of events that can hinder a victim's ability to respond with intimacy in marriage. The potential consequences may include a deterioration of self-concept, learning to use sex as a form of barter, difficulty experiencing sexual arousal within the context of marriage, and pain during intercourse. If this definition is setting off emotional alarms, see the endnotes section at the end of this chapter.[3]

Negative messages about sex

If sexual encounters during childhood and adolescence can set the stage for disturbances in the marital bed, so can years of hearing messages that sex is dirty, loathsome, dangerous, or something that God basically dislikes but tolerates (perhaps turning His gaze away) for the continuation of the human race. A more common scenario involves well-intentioned but overzealous parental efforts to prevent adolescents from embarking on sexual misadventures. If negative messages such as these are impacting the enjoyment of marital sex, they should be identified and addressed. Later in the chapter we'll look at how this repair work can be done.

Sexual wounds sustained during adulthood

Despite the alluring pictures of red-hot, carefree, and uncommitted sexual encounters painted by the media, the reality is that sex, like the relationship in which it occurs, is a living, growing, blooming, maturing entity. It's likely to involve false starts, misfires, mistakes, pleasant interludes, playfulness, passion, and, yes, some fireworks of the good kind. Overall it needs to be planted in good, rich soil—a relationship that is not only fueled by physical and emotional attraction but is also stable, mutually respectful, and deeply committed to the other's well-being. Once planted, it needs to be nurtured, studied, and most of all, handled with care.

Sex outside of marriage. A person whose first sexual encounters occur outside of marriage will nearly always experience a multilayered sense of loss—physically, emotionally, relationally, morally—accompanied by the question, *What does it matter now?* Once that line has been crossed, resistance to more sexual activity is usually seriously weakened. With repeated sexual hookups and breakups comes a sadder (but unfortunately not wiser) conclusion: sex and commitment have nothing in common. As we cautioned earlier, with each disengagement (involving rejection at some level) after a sexual liaison, a piece of innocence is ripped away and replaced by a growing cynicism about the possibility of experiencing a loving, stable, safe, and secure relationship with someone of the opposite sex.

The growing skepticism about the less-than-honorable intentions of the opposite sex is especially significant for women, who more so than men are positioned culturally to use sexuality as their power base. Once a woman is experienced or old enough to know how to be in control of sexual situations, her sexuality may become a tool that she can wield to get what she needs or wants in a relationship. Sex often becomes a form of barter, *both before and after marriage.*

Abortion. With increased frequency of sexual contacts, the risk of an unplanned pregnancy and subsequent abortion escalates, and statistically, young unmarried women are likely to choose abortion to extract themselves from a tight spot. Sadly, the emotional havoc wreaked in the aftermath of an abortion is often inestimable, including profound disruptions in future relationships. If you've experienced an abortion in your past, it's quite possible that unresolved guilt associated with that decision is affecting your present sex life—especially if your spouse was involved in the decision. After many years of counseling women (and men) who have struggled with the aftereffects of abortion, Teri wrote (along with her favorite coauthor) *A Solitary Sorrow* (Random House, 2000), a book that explores the complexities of this heartbreaking life event.

Pornography. It's no secret that men—even those who are deeply committed to expressing their sexuality strictly within the boundaries of marriage—are wired in such a way as to be irresistibly drawn to visual sexual stimuli. Pornography has thus always been a thriving business, but over the past two decades it has become accessible in ways that were barely conceivable a generation ago. This, of course, is the fruit of the Internet, where two mouse clicks can instantly display incredibly graphic material on anyone's computer screen.

By the way, accessing pornography isn't solely a male activity. Women reportedly comprise more than one of four viewers of pornographic material, although in Teri's counseling experience this commonly occurs at the insistence of a male partner who wants to "spice things up." Not surprisingly, however, women who view pornography differ drastically from their male counterparts in that they prefer their "spice" to include a plot involving two people who actually fall in love. (Since men can be stimulated at a moment's notice by images alone, pornographic material geared to them is notoriously idiotic when it comes to plot, character, and dialogue. Women are far more likely to interact with sexually provocative material in the form of steamy romance novels and edgy character-driven stories of the *Sex and the City* genre.)

For the sake of brevity we'll address the most common scenario, which involves a husband accessing porn and a wife who feels rejected and hurt when she discovers his secret. The husband almost always tries in vain to placate his outraged partner by saying that he considers this computer-screen indulgence to have no bearing on his love for his wife. Indeed, he usually truly believes that she "shouldn't take this personally." And, understandably, she usually doesn't buy this explanation.

While the wife is completely justified in feeling betrayed, her husband's use of pornography does indeed have more to do with addiction than judging his partner to be inadequate in the bedroom. Framing the issue in this light can help a couple find healing for this disruptive issue. Like drug addiction, accessing pornography may begin as an experiment to satisfy curiosity (or even an accidental exposure during adolescence), but it can rapidly morph into an internal big black dog that demands to be fed larger helpings more often. Viewing pornography (and experiencing the associated orgasm from masturbation) becomes an effective and readily accessible anxiety reducer. But as with the first rush of cocaine, a powerful neural pathway created in the pleasure center of the brain beckons and then demands that the experience be repeated. And, like drugs, with repeated exposure the user may require more—and more extreme—material to reproduce anything close to that initial high. The behavior that was initially casual and controlled becomes the master of the user, and thus even the most repentant husband who has made a "never again" pledge faces an uphill battle to keep it.

When an addiction to pornography comes to light, specific steps need to be taken to reverse the damage. The couple must be willing to discuss this issue openly and in a matter-of-fact manner. Along with the need to process the great shame on the part of the user and the angry feelings of betrayal on the part of the wife, the healing process also needs to include some straightforward discussion about steps that are necessary for treating *any* form of addiction.

The addict must be willing to set up a system of strict accountability—therapy, a support group, setting up the computer in a way that the wife can access a record of all Web sites her husband visits, and so forth. This does not mean that a wife should become the porn police. The husband's accountability ultimately should be with a trusted male friend, support group, counselor, or pastor (or preferably more than one of these). The purpose of setting up a system on the computer that allows a wife to know what sites have been asccesssed by her husband is twofold: It gives her peace of mind and establishes the beginning of a foundation for rebuilding trust.

Marital counseling will probably be necessary so that both can understand how and why this addiction got started in the first place. The bad news is that all addicts remain vulnerable to whatever they've taught themselves to associate with relief of anxiety. But the good news is that weeds *do* grow over a neural pathway that no longer gets any traffic! Keep in mind, however, that this process typically takes 18 to 24 months of intentional hard work, *so don't give up.*

Having framed pornography as an addiction, we would be remiss if we didn't add that, unlike other kinds of addiction, the habit of using porn has an extremely personal impact on the wife. For one thing she may be asked to perform sexually in ways that are uncomfortable to her. But more important is that a woman feels betrayed (not to mention insulted and degraded) when she believes her husband needs to close his eyes and imagine someone else during sex (usually a young "actress" with a seemingly ferocious appetite for anything and everything sexual).

Healing sexual dysfunction

In an otherwise healthy marital relationship, the request for sex (usually, but not always, on the part of the man as we saw in the sidebar "When the Wife Has More Libido Than Her Husband") can become the source of painful misunderstanding, guilt, anger, shame, and confusion between a husband and wife. Teri spends so much time dealing with sexual problems in marriage that this section could be the length of an epic novel. But writing that version is a future project, and we'll therefore give an extremely brief explanation of her general approach to excavating and dealing with this most tender of marital issues.

Ruling out physiological and/or medical factors for sexual problems. Although most sexual problems in marriage have an emotional and/or psychological basis, there are also possible physiological explanations that need to be ruled out. In women, pain during intercourse might have a physical explanation (vaginal dryness, endometriosis, infection, congenital abnormalities involving the vagina and reproductive organs, injury, etc.). Additionally, women can experience a drastically lowered sex drive during perimenopause and menopause, or after childbirth. Men can experience erectile dysfunction for a number of physical reasons, including diabetes, vascular (blood vessel) disease, surgery, and side effects of medications.

Low libido in both men and women can be a side effect of certain drugs (especially some widely utilized antidepressants and blood-pressure medications), chronic illnesses, and subnormal hormonal levels, to name a few. Smoking, alcoholism, obesity, depression, and anxiety disorders can disrupt normal sexual functioning. So if you're really ready to address this issue in your relationship, it's likely that a medical exam and consultation will be part of the process to make sure all of the puzzle pieces are on the table before attempting to put the whole picture together.

Approaching sexual problems in marriage with a therapist's help. (Or, What really goes on during sex therapy?) The first order of business is to have a frank discussion about the guilt and shame surrounding this topic. The scenario described at the beginning of this chapter—husband wants more frequent and enthusiastic sex than his wife is willing or able to provide—is the most typical one that Teri hears. It's *crucial* to frame this issue with an approach that says, "Okay, we may not be happy with what we've got going in this department, but at least we're not so different from everybody else." The wife has to stop feeling guilty for not being a sex goddess. The husband has to stop feeling like some sort of sex fiend or "dirty old (young) man" because he'd like to have sex with his wife a few times a month. It is what it is, folks. This is the average situation, and not many married couples are thrilled with it. Teri urges couples to start by making a decision to drop the guilt and blame so they can roll up their sleeves and make their sex life *better* than average, because what is "average" in married sex all too often isn't very satisfying for either person.

Creating a road map of sexual wounds for each partner. A thorough excavation of each spouse's history of sexual wounds (including the usual sources of sexual toxicity outlined previously—early sexual abuse, unhealthy messages about sex from the family of origin, and previous sexual relationships in adulthood) doesn't exactly sound like a picnic. Indeed, it isn't.

In fact, it's altogether possible that progress toward improved sexual intimacy in marriage may stall at this point because the husband or wife may feel too ashamed, embarrassed, or traumatized to explore this sensitive subject. But like a thorough history during a medical evaluation, a careful review with a competent and caring therapist is not only helpful but is also necessary to fully understand the extent of each person's sexual wounds and their impact on the marriage. This kind of "excavation" project is usually done individually, apart from the marital sessions, for the sake of protecting one person from having to deal with disturbing mental images relating to the other's prior sexual experiences.

No doubt about it. This is hard work. But so is the process of repairing and restoring any area of life that has sustained damage, and as a result isn't working well (or not at all). Here's a public service announcement: *If you have tough issues in your life, sexual or otherwise, don't put off getting help because you are apprehensive about the work involved to address them.* Teri has found that nearly all couples who are willing to do this work see some degree of improvement in their physical intimacy.

Dealing with the wounds from early negative messages about sex. All parents were once children and then adolescents, and all have had sex, but for some reason most parents have a difficult time educating their children about almost everything having to do with this topic. Often

they shy away from even the most straightforward explanation of reproductive anatomy and functions. Even if they're relaxed about providing
the names and addresses of the basic body parts, the Big Question—
How does the baby get into a mommy's tummy?—continues to generate
sweaty palms, even in our day and age when these topics are discussed
openly in the media.

Then, beyond the generic birds-and-bees stuff comes the challenge
of transmitting healthy information about negotiating the physical
aspects of romantic relationships. Between the extremes—"Don't make
any physical contact at all before your wedding day" at one end, and "I
know you're going to do it, so let's get you some condoms or birth
control pills" at the other—lies what may seem like a high-wire act.
Parents may be scared to death that any discussion of parameters for
physical affection will be perceived by their adolescent as a green light.
They may have done things as teenagers or young adults that they don't
want their kids to know about, either out of their own guilt or a concern that the kids will think, *If Mom and Dad did ___, then they can't
ask me not to go there.* Sadly, to top things off, parents often don't model
healthy physical affection after being married for a couple of decades,
because physical affection ceased long ago.

Even if you're one of the fortunate few raised by parents who trans-
mitted healthy, positive messages about sex, you may not have married
someone who had a positive role model. Whatever your upbringing, it's
so important for both of you to take the time to hear and understand
what the other person "caught" during his or her upbringing about this
subject. All too often, teens emerge into young adulthood burdened
with spoken and (usually) unspoken communications from each parent

that sex is bad and shameful. Though they may make choices to become sexually involved anyway, that parental disapproval or discomfort about sex never detaches from the psyche. It marches straight into the marriage and beyond. This is one of many areas in life where relationships are troubled because of behavior driven by old and unspoken assumptions. When these beliefs are identified and verbalized, both husband and wife are often surprised—but they're also better equipped to make some attitude adjustments that benefit the marriage.

Dealing with sexual wounds sustained in adulthood. This is the most difficult part of creating the road map, because no one likes to hear about a spouse's extracurricular sexual relationships, whether they occurred before or (in the case of affairs) after the marriage. So let's start with a strong warning: Think carefully about how much information you should disclose to your spouse, and how explicit it should be. A detailed account of your prior sexual activities may plant images in your spouse's mind that are likely to be both painful and permanent.

If you have a complex sexual history—especially when it includes previous lovers—you should seriously consider reviewing it privately with a counselor who is competent and experienced in this topic, because your prior sexual history will almost certainly affect your spouse. The counselor can guide you as to how much detail you should disclose. (*Please note:* We're talking about using discretion in recounting graphic details; we're most certainly *not* suggesting you withhold the basic outline of your sexual history, which is vital for your partner to understand as part of knowing who you are. But under no circumstances should you ever compare your spouse's sexual performance unfavorably with that of a previous partner. To do so is cruel, disrespectful, and a surefire way to decrease the likelihood of enthusiastic sex in the future. Even a *favorable* comparison with a previous partner is unwise, because it's likely to bring to your spouse's mind troubling images of your physical intimacy with another person.) The point of going through the potentially shameful exercise of charting the history of sexual involvements is to allow you and your partner to begin to approach this topic with understanding and compassion. If you can hear your spouse articulate the pain of his or her journey, perhaps you can start responding with kindness and expend less (fruitless) energy on feeling the shame and anger of failed expectations.

Talk about it!

Even couples who enjoy talking about everything under the sun may not communicate at all about what goes on between the sheets. Perhaps they're afraid of hurting the other person's feelings, sounding naive, or "talking dirty." They may mistakenly believe that their bodies, or whatever sounds they make during lovemaking, are saying it all.

Talking candidly and carefully about what is and isn't working in the bedroom is an interpersonal skill many couples lack, but it's a skill that needs to be cultivated if this part of your relationship is going to improve. When you like something your spouse does before, during, or after sex, feel free to say so—right away, later, or both. Don't hesitate to be specific: "That really feels good," or "I enjoyed it when you . . ." When you *don't* like something your spouse does before, during, or after sex, you should also say something—but pick the time, place, and words carefully. A critique offered immediately after the fact is likely to be discouraging and may set up an unhealthy performance mode for the other person. Likewise, a disparaging comment about last night's sexual encounter that's tossed into an argument about a different subject is like a verbal hand grenade that will injure rather than inform.

As with all the tough marital issues, a respectful and uncritical hearing of what your spouse honestly wants to say about what happens in the bedroom will almost always (eventually) result in a better relationship. Yes, we know: It's an extremely delicate subject, and the first conversation or two will probably not yield instantaneous harmony. But a continued dialogue usually produces a deeper emotional and sexual intimacy in the long run. We wholeheartedly encourage you to take that risk, because we truly believe you will find the end product to be well worth the effort.

Exercise: Journaling about sexual issues

The following questions are meant to be used for private journaling. You may or may not decide to share your thoughts with your spouse.

1. On a scale of 1 to 10 (with 10 being complete satisfaction), how would you rate the sexual health of your marriage? Explain why you gave this rating.

2. If you experienced a higher satisfaction level at some other time in your marriage, when was that, and what was going on in your lives at that time?

3. When, if ever, have you and your spouse had a productive, respectful talk about your sex life?

4. If you're going through this book with your spouse, try the following: Each of you write down how long it has been since you last had sex. Compare your answers. If there is a discrepancy in your recollection—and there usually will be—discuss what the possible reasons might be.

Endnotes

1. Robert T. Michael et al., *Sex in America: A Definitive Survey* (Boston: Little, Brown, 1994), 124.

2. Diane Mandt Langberg, *On the Threshold of Hope: Opening the Door to Healing for Survivors of Sexual Abuse* (Carol Stream, IL: Tyndale House, 1999), 43–44.

3. Teri recommends Diane Langberg's *On the Threshold of Hope: Opening the Door to Healing for Survivors of Sexual Abuse* (Carol Stream, IL:Tyndale, 1999) and Dan Allender's *The Wounded Heart: Hope for Adult Victims of Childhood Sexual Abuse* (Colorado Springs, CO: NavPress, 2008). The book Teri almost always has her clients read is a by non-Christian author Judith Herman, *Trauma and Recovery: The Aftermath of Violence* (New York: Basic Books, 1997). The best Bible study Teri has ever seen/used on early sexual abuse is Linda Cochrane's *The Path to Sexual Healing* (Grand Rapids, MI: Baker Books, 2000).

6

Finances in Flux

It used to be said that if something were reliable and trustworthy you
could "take it to the bank." As the first decade of the twenty-first century sputtered to a close, many people no doubt considered revising
that well-worn expression to "You can stuff it in your mattress." Indeed,
if current events have taught us anything, it should be that the flow of
money in and out of our hands, bank accounts, and portfolios is hardly
predictable.

Numerous studies have confirmed that money is a common subject for combat among married couples. Interestingly, money isn't the
number-one reason for divorce. Individuals most often cite dissatisfaction with the marriage itself as the reason for exiting. This is why we
consider the acquisition of a communication skill set to be of such
incredible importance. Even if one or both of you were born with the
proverbial silver spoon firmly implanted, finances will be a stress point
for every couple at some time. The big question is not *whether* there will

be fights about money, but *how* those heated discussions will be resolved. For example, in 2004 more than a thousand couples were interviewed regarding how finances impacted their relationship.[1] Let's see how you and your spouse compare with the findings:

- Seventy percent of the couples reported that they *talked* about money each week, but without necessarily taking the high ground needed to partner successfully in finances (or anything else). Of those surveyed, 36 percent of the men and 40 percent of the women admitted that they had lied to their spouse about the cost of a purchase.

- Most money fights were about debt and spousal spending— especially spending on children, and *especially* in a blended-family situation.

- Two-thirds of the men earned more than their partners, and 32 percent of men felt they had more say in financial issues (compared to 22 percent of women). However, women were more likely to feel that they "win" money fights.

- Fourteen percent of the women admitted to withholding sex after this kind of fight, compared to 5 percent of the men. (We wonder if the actual figure was 0.005 percent of the men.)

- Both men and women confessed that the financial topic that worried them most was being unprepared for retirement.

- Forty-one percent of men and 32 percent of women paid off their credit cards monthly.

Here's a plotline that Teri has watched unfold in the counseling office on a regular basis. In the beginning, starry-eyed engaged couples usually don't worry too much about their future finances. One reason is that they're thinking mostly about having sex. "We'll live on love," they gush to each other, and they're partly right. When things settle down after the honeymoon, there usually isn't much to fight about in the financial department because there isn't that much money to work with, and it has to cover the basics: rent, food, transportation, and so on. There's usually a definite feeling that any income is "our money," and there's not a lot of room for hiding it or making unilateral spending decisions. There's also a lot of sex, which can make up for not having a lot of money.

After a few years, husband and wife are often spending a fair amount of their day engaged in activities that don't involve the other. If they're both earning an income, more likely than not they do so in separate workplaces. If there are infants and toddlers running around the house, usually the wife is spending more of her time tending to them while the husband is spending more of his time earning a living. In the financial realm, one of two patterns tends to develop at this stage. The least common (by a long shot) is that there develops mutual accountability and collaboration regarding the use of money. The need for a budget—that is, a deliberate understanding of the amounts of family income going to various destinations—is recognized and discussed and then consistently implemented, regardless of who actually pays the bills every month. If this is what you did from the outset of your marriage, or even after several years of wandering in the financial wilderness, congratulations. For the other 99.9 percent of you, the following scenario may sound more familiar.

Typically, one member of the couple is better at record keeping and therefore becomes the designated bill payer. However, the couple fails to develop an intentional approach for mutual accountability and responsibility. Without ongoing collaboration it becomes difficult to say no when one or the other wants to buy something, because there's no plan and no mechanism for assessing the request. The bill payer— who starts with what should be only an administrative role—gradually assumes more decision-making power by default. Indeed, that person often feels reticent to relinquish the chief-financial-officer role, because it can be enjoyable to have some independence in making spending decisions. But he or she will also feel the heat when money becomes tight. The spouse who isn't paying close attention to the money situation may make matters worse by engaging in some spending that unknowingly puts the couple deeper in the financial hole. Resentment may fester in the spouse who is lying awake at night, fretful over unpaid bills and irritated at a snoozing bedmate who is getting off easy. He or she may try to impose some spending limits or allowances on the other, usually finding little joy in the role of money cop. The other is likely to be equally irritated over feeling relegated to a childlike position when it comes to financial decisions.

Whether or not the money-managing roles shift in your marriage, we can almost guarantee that your financial fortunes will change over time. What might happen when your ship comes in— or sinks? *Either* of these situations has the potential to enhance or undermine a marriage, depending on several factors, including . . . guess what? That's right: communication patterns, family-of-origin patterns, self-worth issues, and all the other stuff we went over earlier in this book.

How financial gains and losses change a marriage

Paul has long been a quiz-show fan and has been a contestant three times, with varying degrees of success.* He'd be lying if he didn't admit that there's a definite rush generated by spending some time in a TV studio and coming home a few thousand dollars richer. He can also vouch for the massive letdown when another contestant ends your winning streak: It's "Hero to Zero" in a flash. Over and above the thrill of victory and the agony of defeat, he can say without question that windfalls such as these don't result in lifelong bliss or financial freedom. Even a major influx—a six-figure inheritance, for example—would appear to promise smooth financial sailing. In fact, it won't guarantee an end to marital issues regarding money.

Although it's true that more cash in the bank may decrease the number of fights about money running out (at least for a while), there are more than a few downsides to this state of affairs. First, as the "lifestyles of the rich, famous, and miserable" regularly attest, money can't guarantee happiness. Writer and comedian Spike Milligan famously quipped that "money can't buy you happiness, but it does bring you a more pleasant form of misery." The depression, drugs, divorces, and downhill slides of many celebrities aren't just tabloid fodder, and they aren't limited to wealthy people in the public eye.

---

* For the record, these were *Tic-Tac-Dough*, *Sale of the Century*, and *Jeopardy*. Paul has steered clear of shows that seem to involve blind luck or exuberant responses, as occurs when the announcer on *The Price Is Right* calls out, "John Doe, come on down!" Upon hearing his name called, John Doe's reaction typically borders on hysteria, even though he hasn't actually won anything.

Another downside to having lots of money is that no matter how much you have, you can still spend more than you make. Our state and federal governments regularly confirm this truism. For some additional spectacular examples, search the term "lottery winners broke" on the Internet and behold the sad stories of fortunes won and lost, usually within just a few years.

A third downside is that a married couple with an abundance of funds may feel less need to collaborate about their financial decisions, although in reality careful decision making is as important (if not more so) when the storehouse is full than when it's bare. Not only are they responsible for using their abundant resources wisely, but those with a lot of money can also become enmeshed in bigger debts or higher-stakes investments—with much greater risk for financial catastrophe—than those with limited funds. A big loss can be particularly devastating when one hasn't informed his or her spouse about the financial (mis)adventure that is now coming home to roost.

When there's a lot of cash in the marital till, there may be far less appreciation for gifts and special events that would be magical in the presence of scarcity. For our first Christmas as a married couple, Paul bought Teri a framed artwork print that she loved. It cost $50—a goodly chunk of Paul's paycheck as a family practice resident in the mid-1970s—and meant a lot to her. Indeed, it still hangs over our bed and generates fond memories more than three decades later.

Another scenario that Teri has seen many times in the counseling office (and experienced) involves a wife who goes back to work after several years of caring for small children at home. Her husband has been plugging away at his workplace, perhaps thinking that his is the harder of the two roles (not!) and almost certainly not appreciating how her confi-

dence in her own abilities may have been dwindling. With her first paycheck may come a major boost in self-confidence—especially if she can use
it to buy a special item that was previously out of reach. If she's in a difficult marriage, the additional money and independence may encourage
her to think about leaving her spouse. Even in a good marriage where the
extra income is welcomed and celebrated, there will be a gravitational pull
on her earnings away from a rainy-day cushion or an ongoing fun-money
stash and toward the black hole of her family's financial obligations.

How do financial losses change a marriage? You probably don't
need to think too hard about this one. Because needs and wants exceed
income at any given time for 99.99 percent of the human race, because
expenses have a way of increasing over the life of a marriage, because
most couples don't collaborate on spending priorities, because credit
cards are so readily available, because of _____ (you fill in the blank),
most couples experience stress and conflict over finances for at least
some of their married life. For many, money fights are a routine occur-
rence—and that's when there are one or two steady paychecks. Throw
a pay cut or job loss into the equation, and things can get dicey in a
hurry. What happens all too often is that each person blames the other
for whatever financial storm is currently battering the home. "If you
made more . . ." squares off against "If you didn't spend so much . . ."

Money talk (or lack thereof)

Like sex, money is a difficult subject for most couples to talk about, and
one big reason is that both topics have great potential to be sources of
deep-seated shame and guilt. These negative emotions have a way of
driving arguments about money way off-road because they keep each

person busy vigorously defending his or her position. No energy or space is available to offer the other person the benefit of the doubt, let alone help clarify and restate his or her own issues in a healthy way. So the average "discussion" about money during any given week usually takes place between two exhausted people late at night and goes something like this:

"Hey! How come there's no money in the account? I need some cash for the trip tomorrow."

"Well, I had to pay bills today. We're already overdue on everything, and I couldn't wait any longer. You'll just have to spend less this time."

"Are you serious? Can I use one of the credit cards, or do you have those all maxed out?"

"You know good and well you use those cards more than I do, so you should know better than I do if they're maxed out! *And* you never showed me how to use the Web site like you said you would, so how am I supposed to know?"

"Yeah, I *should* know, because they were *supposed* to be just for my business travel, but you kind of blew that to smithereens, didn't you?"

"Well, if you made more money, I wouldn't have to resort to using the cards, now would I? What happened to that *fabulous* raise you were promised last year?"

"I make more than any of my friends (and I'm really tired of feeling no appreciation from you, by the way), so my income isn't the problem here. If you can't control your charging, I'm going to just take away the cards."

"Oh, really? How old *are* we right now? You can't balance the checkbook to save your life, so I guess you're in no position to try that power trip, bucko. Honestly, you are being so ridiculous right now!"

"Seriously, your spending is out of control. You're going to have to stop buying so much for the kids. You'll never catch up with your sister; I wish you'd quit trying to impress her!"

"You have got to be kidding me. As I recall, *you* were the one who completely derailed our finances last year with that danged boat you just *had* to have for your brother's visit!"

"Fine. Whatever. I'm going to finish packing."

End of scene. Cut. Print.

Lest you think this exchange involves a lot of dramatic license, scenes like this have been played out nearly verbatim in Teri's office. And every time an unhealthy clash like this happens, there's zero progress toward finding a collaborative solution to the issue of the mysteriously dipping bank account, but there *is* a hefty deposit made in the bank that holds all the feelings of hurt and betrayal. At the end of the encounter, each person feels unheard, blamed, and disrespected. Even worse, all the shame that goes along with "Why can't I handle money correctly?" is activated. But there's no possibility for the shame to be fully investigated, because each person uses any previous admission of mistakes on the other spouse's part as a weapon to be wielded without mercy in the argument.

Here's an alternative version of this exchange that we might call Teri's ideal director's cut of the same scene with a new script:

"Hey! How come there's no money in the account? I need some cash for the trip tomorrow."

"Well, I had to pay bills today. We're already overdue on everything, and I couldn't wait any longer. How much do you think you'll need?"

"Yikes. Unfortunately, this trip is a little more involved. How's the balance on the credit cards?"

"I'm not sure. I could check, but I have to confess I still haven't figured out how to access the site online."

"Yeeaah . . . we've kind of messed up, because I got those two cards so I could keep business expenses separated."

"I know, I know. I feel really guilty about that. I shouldn't be using them, but it's just too tempting when there's no money in the account and the kids need something. I think I justify it to myself because I'm assuming that when the raise comes through, it'll be retroactive, and then we can zero out these balances and use the cards just for business after that."

"And I feel guilty because I just pretty much have my head in the sand about where we are financially, while you're stuck trying to make it all stretch somehow. I don't like the way this feels."

"Me, neither. It's kind of a relief to be talking about this. I've been so stressed out. I try to protect you from worrying about the bounced checks because I know you've got your hands full at work, but after a while, it starts to feel like I'm the one doing all the worrying. I know that's not true, but sometimes when I'm paying the bills, I feel pretty alone in this mess."

Silence.

"Okay, I don't like it that you're feeling that way. This is *our* mess together. I think we need to make some time to talk this through and fix it. Obviously, we can't do much with this tonight, but how about this Saturday? We could send the kids over to your sister's and spend the afternoon looking at all this."

"That would be such a relief. Yeah, I'd like that very much."

This may sound like fantasyland compared to what goes on in your home, but Teri spends a good deal of time in her office with an imaginary referee's whistle, coaching couples to keep redoing a fight until it looks something like this. Why bother? Because the new-and-improved exchange concludes with each person feeling heard, understood, and not judged by the other. Most important, heads have been removed from the sand, and shame about money issues has been activated, but with an important difference: There is now some hope that the shame can finally be dealt with. A game plan has been made, and each spouse begins to think, *Maybe I can finally change how I deal with money without always coming to a dead end marked "You're a hopeless idiot!" Maybe I can finally see some forward movement on this issue and stop condemning myself.*

Oh no . . . Please don't say the b word!

When the couple in the previous section ends their "come to Jesus" meeting* on Saturday, we hope they'll have identified the one single

---

* Originally used in the 1991 film *Flight of the Intruder* in the court-martial scene, this phrase has come to describe a straight and honest talk that includes hearing an ego-bruising truth, confessing, and repenting. It also carries an emotional resolve to live one's life differently in the future.

most important tool that must be established to take the fight out of money issues: *the dreaded budget.*

The answer to resolving all issues about money in a marital civilization is so stunningly simple that it never ceases to amaze us that so few couples ever implement it! Of course, this may seem like saying to someone who has battled the scale for years, "You want to lose weight? It's simple: Eat less food!" No one wants to be told to eat less or spend less, because gratification derived from eating or spending money is usually so immediate and soothing. And the more unpleasant and chaotic one's life, the more soothing one needs in order to avoid thinking about all that is unpleasant and chaotic. A budget, like a diet, screams of deprivation and punishment, and most of us are simply not willing to restrict our "right" to feel good *now.* The drive to have our anxiety soothed without delay seems to trump our ability to think about a better way to live in the long run.

Here are two examples that show the utter magic of a budget. We're hoping they sound intriguing enough to entice you to go through the hard work of setting one up.

Example 1—Setup for a marital storm. You desperately want that new 65-inch flat-screen TV, but you know your wife is going to dig in her heels because she thinks the old, boxy 27-inch set is perfectly adequate, and the money shouldn't be spent frivolously just because your guy friends are raving about the glories of football games in high-definition.

But you avoid the marital storm because you've already discussed your need for electronic gadgetry with your wife—watching sports is your primary form of decompression after a hard day, and the quality of picture and sound seriously enhances these time-outs—and you've successfully factored this into your family budget negotiations. There is now a line item on the budget for your electronic toys. Remembering that you've been denying yourself new gadgetry for 10 months, you look at the year-to-date budget numbers. Lo and behold, by waiting for your monthly "toy allowance" to accrue, you have more than enough to justify buying the new television! This assumes, of course, that (1) the two of you have actually kept within the budget guidelines, and (2) there aren't any unforeseen financial emergencies floating around that trump your "right" to spend your toy allowance because the emergency-savings fund hasn't yet had time to build up.

You can joyously let your spouse know you'll be picking up the new set this afternoon. She'll shrug, utterly mystified as to why this would induce such euphoria, but there shouldn't be a fight over the purchase, because it has been provided for in a budget that was previously agreed upon by both partners!

Example 2—Setup for a marital storm. The car needs new brakes, you just found out you need a root canal, and your health insurance company has just cheerfully informed you that you owe a four-figure deductible for your son's recent trip to the emergency room for a broken arm, courtesy of his skateboard. You grit your teeth because you know what always happens: When several unexpected bills converge at the same time, you and your spouse lose that lovin' feeling. Each of you blames the other for the sad refrain that there's never quite enough to get ahead of the curve. This is particularly unpleasant because you'd been planning a romantic weekend at a bed-and-breakfast up the coast—without the kids—for the first time in five years.

But you avoid the marital storm because the budget you and your spouse set up a year ago included an automatic deduction of 10 percent to go directly into savings, and you now have an emergency fund that can take the impact of the unplanned bills. It's a bummer that the nest egg now has to be reduced so drastically, but because the car, dental, and medical bills can be paid without disrupting the monthly budget, you and your sweetie can enjoy that lovely weekend away, as planned, without blame or shame about financial chaos. What a concept!

The principles of a working budget are pretty basic: (1) Don't spend more than you earn, and (2) slowly build up a reserve so that emergencies don't derail your budget. So if the answer to ending all fights about money forever is to simply create and live by a balanced budget, *why don't we all just do it?*

What stops us from talking about a budget?

There are many factors that can prevent us from having healthy dialogues about money. Lack of collaboration about money may be a symptom of a greater problem—an absence of trust and intimacy in the marriage on all subjects, money included. Or maybe one of you uses retail therapy to self-soothe, and there's a conscious or unconscious motivation *not* to be accountable to a spouse for fear of losing access to that addiction. (Teri has noted an alarming trend among married people: acquiring individual credit cards and not informing one's spouse.)

Maybe your family's income stream is variable, and you've never been taught how to establish a working budget under these conditions. (It *can* be done.) As we've already stated, though, the main reason couples don't create a budget is because there's such a sense of personal failure and shame surrounding the issue of money, and it's just plain miserable to talk about it aloud.

Most important, we all heard messages about the meaning of money from our parents, whether or not they deliberately taught us how to manage it. And those beliefs, whether or not you agree with them, may have been unwittingly carried from your old civilization into your marriage. Understanding what came in attached like a stowaway is an important step to taking the fight out of money issues (see "Meeting no. 1: Understanding each other's beliefs about money" later in this chapter).

Fixing the financial problem

The first step toward resolving money issues in your marriage is the most difficult: raising the white flag of surrender, coming to the middle of the battlefield, and agreeing that a truce must be implemented in order to negotiate a treaty. If feelings haven't been too badly mangled over the years by accusations and counterattacks, you might be able to work through the process on your own. Or you might need the help of a third party, such as a financial planner or a marriage therapist. We highly recommend the accountability of a Crown Financial Ministries[2] small group.

Reviving a sinking economy takes time in civilizations both large and small. If it took years to create the mess you're in, don't expect to clean it up overnight. The process of creating financial order from chaos involves several stages over a period of time. If you're serious about *finally* addressing this area of your marriage, you'll need to set aside an hour a week on a regular basis for a while. Without an intentional, regular meeting time, this simply isn't going to happen, because one or both of you will find every excuse under the sun *not* to talk about money. Once the budget is set in place, a monthly review will probably suffice to keep things on track. Needless to say, these meeting times need to be utterly protected from interruption and distraction. Buckle up—it could get bumpy.

Meeting no. 1: Understanding each other's beliefs about money

Your first financial meeting needs to be completely unthreatening, so *numbers should not be brought to the table.* As with virtually every issue we've addressed in this book, an eyes-wide-open look at how you grew up is the starting place for understanding how you react in various situations.

Humans in general react to situations based on assumptions about the way the world works. If you haven't taken the time to examine those foundational beliefs, you may be wholly unaware of them. You may even be functioning based on principles that you don't even consciously agree with anymore. And if *you* don't know why you feel and act the way you do, the chances are slim indeed that your spouse will miraculously ferret out this information.

Prior to the first meeting, each person needs to look at the following list of common beliefs about money. (This is hardly a comprehensive list. If these statements don't accurately represent your attitudes, you can modify them or write some of your own.) Put a check mark next to the ones that seem to describe your true beliefs about money (whether you like them or not), and then circle three that are particularly important in your mental-emotional economy, so to speak. When you sit down together, compare notes and see what you learn about your spouse, and most likely his or her family of origin as well.

____ Whoever makes the money holds the power.

____ Whoever makes the money controls financial decisions.

____ It's virtuous to be poor.

____ The only real security in life is having a lot of money.

____ Only rich people are respected.

____ A husband's job is to bring home a paycheck.

____ A wife's job is to figure out how to make the paycheck stretch.

____ Time is money.

____ If you love someone, you buy them things.

____ Ain't no such thing as a free lunch, baby!

____ If you love me, you'll prove it by buying me things.

____ In marriage, no matter who earns what, it's our money together.

____ Only an idiot pays retail.

____ Women shouldn't have to worry about money.

____ In every marriage, there's a spender and a saver. Period.

____ An adult shouldn't have to account to a spouse for every penny spent.

____ You can't take it with you; money should be spent!

____ Impulsive spending is the best kind of spending.

____ Rich people are snobs.

____ I'd be happy if I had enough money.

____ Money isn't spiritual.

____ I can't hold on to money.

____ Accepting money obligates you.

___ Rich people are dishonest and greedy.

___ This is as good as it's going to get for me financially.

___ I don't want the responsibility of a lot of money.

___ People like me don't succeed financially.

___ You can't have both time and money.

___ Never buy top-of-the-line items.

___ If I make more than my folks did, I would feel as if I were betraying them.

___ I don't want to be the richest of my friends.

___ I don't want to be the poorest of my friends.

___ I don't deserve a lot of money.

___ It's not fair that other people have more money than I do.

___ Money corrupts.

___ If I spend money on something that doesn't work out, I'm stupid.

___ I need only enough money to get by.

___ The first 10 percent of every paycheck belongs to God.

___ The first 10 percent of every paycheck goes into savings.

___ I can give to church and charities once I've got my bills paid.

___ If I had a lot of money, I'd never know who *really* liked me.

___ Worrying about money is vulgar.

___ Trying to live within a budget just sets you up to fail.

(Add your own)

_____

The most important aspect of this meeting is that it does *not* include any accusations, reprimands, or lectures ("Aha! So you finally admit that *you* are to blame for this mess!"). The goals of this first meeting are (1) to allow yourself, perhaps for the first time in your life, to go inside and seriously explore your relationship with money, and (2) to have that excavation fully heard by your spouse—without being told you're bad or wrong for carrying those attitudes into the marriage. The purpose is to understand how each of you thinks about money so that you can decide if you *like* how you think or if you want to establish some new operating principles together.

Meeting no. 2: Defining the problem

Use this second meeting as an opportunity to do something you may never have done before with the issue of money: As dispassionately as a relentless Sherlock Holmes, find answers without blame or shame. If you can tell yourself and each other the unvarnished truth about how you created this present situation *together*, then doing the hard work of turning it all around can become a masterpiece of collaboration rather than a tangled mass of resentment and guilt (which will only guarantee failure). According to financial advisor Ruth Hayden, author of *For Richer, Not Poorer*, husbands and wives usually spend about the same amount of money. Men tend to make fewer but more expensive purchases, whereas women spend more often on smaller ticket items. To turn your financial ship around, the following steps are essential:

1. *Align your values about finances.* Your present values are based on those basic beliefs about money that you caught from your parents. Review the following list, and put a check mark next to one of the following statements in each grouping that best describes your preference; then compare your answers with your spouse. *Choose the answer you*

honestly feel is more important, whether or not it's presently being done. Notice that a legitimate case can be made for either side. There are no right or wrong answers, just opinions based on personal values.

Which is more important to you?

____ Building a fat, secure savings account OR

____ "Seizing the day" and enjoying the journey

____ Paying off credit-card balances every month OR

____ Paying the minimum monthly payment, plus a little

____ A trip to Maui OR

____ Having the front yard professionally landscaped

____ Saving to put the kids through college OR

____ Allowing them to value their education more by paying for it themselves

____ Maximum insurance OR

____ Minimum insurance

____ Individual checking accounts OR

____ A joint checking account

____ Balancing the checkbook to the penny (one hour) OR

____ Balancing the checkbook to within $10.00 (10 minutes)

____ Having one parent at home full time OR

____ Both parents contributing to the family income

____ Giving kids allowance based on household chores OR

____ Giving kids an automatic allowance so they learn to manage spending

____ Turning out all lights that aren't currently in use OR

____ Judging the pennies saved to be of little significance in the long run

____ Willingness to make a spontaneous big-ticket purchase on a spectacular deal OR

____ Willingness to make a large purchase only if it has been planned

____ Paying the bills early OR

____ Waiting as long as possible to pay a bill to keep the money in the bank

____ Working at a low-paying job I love OR

____ Working at a high-paying job I don't enjoy as much

____ Borrowing money from family if interest can be avoided OR

____ Borrowing money only from a bank and not involving family

____ Putting money in high-risk, high-return investments OR

____ Putting money in low-risk, moderate-return investments

Before you compare your answers, go back and read the paragraph at the end of "Meeting no. 1." All of these exercises will put your communication skills from chapter 3 to the test. For example, for years we butted heads about the types and quantities of insurance we should have. Paul leaned heavily toward insuring against every possible type of loss, including damage to our property from elephant stampedes and invaders from Mars. Teri resented seeing money fly away every month for premiums on policies we never seemed to use. Several conversations were necessary for Teri to understand how insurance buffered Paul's angst over protecting the family and home, and for Paul to understand Teri's frustration over money seemingly flowing down the insurance drain that could have been spent on something more tangible. Compromises—for example, agreeing to take a higher deductible to reduce a premium, rather than getting rid of a particular policy altogether—were often necessary. But the primary value of the conversations was learning how the other person felt and then finding common ground from which to make decisions.

2. *Identify the dynamic that put you here.* So far, we've given you a structured dialogue that's carefully designed to allow some conversation while avoiding finger-pointing. At some point, however, there has to be a clear-eyed yet compassionate look at how the present financial situation was created. If the preceding exercises haven't put you both in a place of hopefulness and mutual generosity of spirit, *do not proceed with this step.* Rather, go back and stay in the previous conversations until you can come to this next phase with both hearts prepared to focus on plugging leaks and bailing water rather than wasting energy on mutual condemnation while the ship is sinking.

If you're ready to continue, take a deep breath, look at the following list, and check off the factors that you believe exist in your situation. Then rank what you consider to be the top three and compare them with your spouse. (As always, the list is not comprehensive. Use the blank spaces at the end to describe anything that pertains to your particular situation.)

____ Impulsive spending by one or both partners

____ Lack of thinking about future financial goals

____ Significant differences in our philosophy of money

___ Financial chaos reflecting an overall lack of marital collaboration

___ Resistance by one or both partners to creating a budget

___ Money secrets (shopping, investments, gambling, etc.)

___ Unrealistic financial goals that doomed us to failure

___ Needing to keep up with the Joneses

___ Spending as a way to self-soothe during times of stress

___ Misuse of credit cards

___ Overspending on children

___ Disagreements about helping relatives and friends financially

___ Not seeing all income, regardless of the source, as "our" money

___ Lack of a system for tracking finances

___ Unwillingness to delay gratification by saving up for something

___ One or both partners trying to control finances

___ Unwillingness to check with partner before making a large purchase

___ Separate checking accounts

___ One person brought more debt into the marriage than the other

___ No savings account was built up to handle emergencies

___ Significant difference in our willingness to take financial risks

___ Strong avoidance of talking about money problems

___ (Add your own.) _____

Before you compare answers with your spouse, take this dire warning seriously: If you honestly feel that your partner bears primary responsibility for the financial bedlam, you'd better figure out a compassionate and generous way to express that opinion if you truly want to fix this problem. You'll need to find a way to convey the following: "I honestly have to tell you that on this particular issue, I don't feel we're equally to blame, and I hope you can hear this without getting defensive. I'll admit to more than 50 percent of the blame on some other issues, but not this one. If you do agree, I promise I won't rub it in, because I don't want that 'morally superior' attitude from *you* when we're discussing another issue where I am more at fault. I don't want either one of us to shame the other—we do that to ourselves just fine already—I just want to look at this honestly and fix it."

3. Allow yourselves to actually look at the numbers. This is possibly the hardest part of turning this painful state of affairs around: You must come out of your denial and actually look at the numbers. This step is so shameful for most people that it may have been years since they've taken their heads out of the sand to take a clear-eyed look at the reality of the financial situation.

List all your debts. *Ack!* Start with what is owed on your home and go from there. *Everything*—credit-card debt, school loans, old debts, back taxes, your parents' "Oh, just pay it back when you can" loan that you've never taken seriously. Subtract the mortgage payment (because that's usually a long-term loan), and total everything else. How much is the monthly interest on that debt costing you? (This could take awhile to calculate.) Is it shocking? Do you have a concrete plan to make that number disappear so you can use that interest payment for something more fun? Do you think the interest payment is going up or down?

If you're paying the minimum payment on your credit cards, we guarantee you're becoming more and more indebted each month. Wouldn't it feel good to have your credit cards at a zero balance every month? Wouldn't it be lovely to climb out of the sinkhole, fill it in, and then pave it over so that you never have to deal with it again? Wouldn't that be worth some effort?

4. *Determine what you're willing to do about the situation.* So we've had a full confession, and we both feel horrified about the bottom line. But we're relieved to have it out in the open. Now what? *The creation of a budget is a nonnegotiable.* But what else might need to happen? This is the time for a freewheeling discussion of all possible actions. No idea should be automatically dismissed. Depending on how dire the situation is—is the ship leaking ominously, or has everything but the last two inches of the upper deck already gone down?—you may have to consider drastic measures, such as completely changing your lifestyle (for example, downsizing to a home you can afford, driving a much cheaper car, giving up the vacation in Maui, or asking the kids to take out college loans). You cannot yet decide what you *need* to do (because you haven't yet created a budget to see what's possible), but this is a time to put all possible solutions on the table without criticism or outright rejection and decide what you're *willing* to do.

Meeting no. 3 (and 4, 5, 6): Creating a balanced budget

Creating a budget is a multistep task, and the process is covered thoroughly in many good books and Web sites, so we won't be taking you through the details of how to do this. It will take a month or two to go back through checkbook registers, credit-card statements, and bank statements to find out where the money has actually gone. Because this can be a thoroughly dismal experience, the chances of completing it go up significantly if both of you keep accountable to a third party (a pastor, a financial counselor,* a therapist, or a small-group study such as one provided by Crown Financial Ministries. The two of you have many decisions to make:

1. *How fast are we willing to pay off this debt?* Budgets that are too aggressive with debt repayment and don't allow for any fun spending are usually doomed to failure. They are the financial equivalent of a crash diet: They take a lot of energy to maintain and thus are rarely sustained long enough to bring about lasting change.

2. *What happens if we can't create a balanced budget?* If the dismal bottom line is that you simply don't make enough money to cover even the nonnegotiable items—mortgage, food, insurance, and so on—you'll probably have to face making some drastic changes in lifestyle.

3. *If we've historically maintained separate finances, do we need to change the system in order to work collaboratively?* It seems to work best to have a single household account if there is only

---

* Note that there are two basic scenarios involving financial planners. Some are consultants who charge by the hour for their services and literally have nothing to sell you. Others analyze your situation and in addition have various investment products (such as mutual funds, stocks, or life insurance) to offer, for which they receive a commission. The latter aren't necessarily going to offer you bad advice—in fact, what they map out may be very wise and prudent—but they may not be entirely even-handed about all of your options. In such cases you may want to get a second opinion before you embark on a course that involves significant amounts of money changing hands.

one wage earner in the home. If both husband and wife earn a paycheck, you can either dump both incomes into a single checking account, or each can have an individual account that feeds a joint household account that is used for handling the household budget. The only thing that will *not* work is maintaining a philosophy of "my money/your money."

4. *Who's going to maintain the system?* The one actually writing the checks and paying bills often begins to resent feeling solely responsible. While doing the actual paperwork is usually assigned to one partner, it's critical that both members are taking responsibility for the financial planning.

5. *How will we know if we're on track with the plan?* It will probably take a couple of months of weekly meetings to set this up. Thereafter, you'll need a monthly state-of-the-union meeting.

The long haul

Though you may have to take the starvation-diet approach initially to save the ship from sinking, maintaining guiltless finances is a lifelong journey. Like lawns and relationships, you can't whip your finances into shape and then forget about them. We speak from plenty of experience. Managing our money, along with dealing with marginless lifestyles (see chapter 4), has been a persistent and recurring challenge in our marriage. Indeed, finances are one of life's areas that are tied to the much larger issue of self-regulation, the willingness to discipline oneself in order to have the greatest possible freedom.

We sincerely hope that you will join us in taking on this challenge.

Exercise: Did you skip this chapter?

If you actually did all the exercises contained in this chapter, you should be pretty much drained. Congratulations—no more questions! Proceed to the next chapter!

If you skimmed over this chapter, you either have your financial act completely together or, more likely, the whole issue of financial management is just too painful to approach. If this is the case, you and your spouse need to make a really big pot of coffee and ask each other one basic question: *What would it take for us to be able to honestly go through this chapter together?*

Endnotes

1. Jena McGregor, "Love and Money," SmartMoney, February 9, 2004, http://www.smartmoney.com/personal-finance/marriage-divorce/Love-Money-15383/

2. For more information, visit the Crown Financial Ministries Web site at www.crown.org. We highly recommend the resources—especially the 10-week small-group study for couples who are ready to take this particular bull by the horns.

7

After the Honeymoon: Years 0 Through 5

> The honeymoon is not actually over until
> we cease to stifle our sighs and begin to
> stifle our yawns.
>
> —widely attributed to Helen Rowland, 20th-century
> American journalist and humorist

The honeymoon's over. So says the phrase that implies that fun is done, and reality is setting in. More ominous is the undertone that a fleeting season of love and acceptance is yielding to a more persistent time of discord and criticism.

Why does the honeymoon have to end? Even if you had the resources to park yourselves permanently at a lovely resort after your wedding day, sipping drinks adorned with little umbrellas and never bothering with minor details like earning a living, running errands, or keeping your place clean, the honeymoon would still be over eventually. And that's a good thing, believe it or not.

In chapter 1 we described the power of "falling in love" and the early phases of a relationship that lead to a profound and satisfying sense of intimacy—the emotional rather than the sexual type. In the last of these phases, we noted that "in this gloriously untested state of rapport, the relationship is idealized, because flaws have yet to be divulged, discovered, or acknowledged. Each has finally found the 'perfect' person."

What happens in the first few years of a marriage is an entirely normal and predictable process in which rapport is tested, without exception. Cracks appear in the veneer of the idealized relationship. Flaws are divulged, discovered, and (reluctantly) acknowledged. Superman turns out to be Clark Kent. Wonder Woman loses her golden lasso. Prince Charming has bad breath. Cinderella has PMS.

Now here's the *really* important part. Indeed, if you don't get anything else from this chapter or, for that matter, this whole book, *now hear this*: Before, during, or shortly after the honeymoon, the relationship turns a critical corner. During the time of courtship and falling in love, both bride- and groom-to-be are working overtime to figure out how to make the other person happy. This is, alas, not the normal orientation or instinct of human beings. Once that blissful period ends, *the natural bent of each person is to begin looking out for his or her own interests*. Whether you believe this arises from genetics, social conditioning, or the fall of humankind, it can be readily confirmed through everyday experience (not to mention the busy schedules of competent marriage and family therapists).

The pull toward looking out for number one is as persistent and relentless as the force of gravity. At some stages of life (for example, toddlerhood), and for some people throughout their lives, its force is routinely on spectacular display. No one is immune to it. While most of us learn to manage its more blatant manifestations as we mature, the one arena where it will not be ignored is within the close physical and emotional quarters of marriage.

This is bad news and good news. The bad news is that, left unattended, self-interest played out in the details of everyday life will obstruct and erode intimacy between two people who once vowed to love, honor, and cherish each other. The wedge may be imperceptible at first and then gradually widen, or it may drive itself into the relationship like a Mack truck, especially if one person is desperately seeking self-worth, as we described in chapter 4. Even when both husband and wife are mature, stable, and well intentioned, this continental drift away from knowing and being known will eventually happen over time unless they take deliberate steps to prevent it.

The good news is that if you're willing to do the work, invest in the relationship, be intentional, be a grown-up, and come to terms with the way things are, you can have the type of intimacy that took your breath away early in your relationship. But this time it will be a hundred times more meaningful, because it's persistent, tested, and authentic rather than based on the euphoria of the courtship bubble (which includes denial and anxiety over "How long can I keep this image up?" or "When will he or she find out who I really am?").

Here's another way of looking at it: Your spouse isn't the person you married, and your marriage isn't the same entity it was on your wedding day. At any given time your marriage is growing warmer or colder. The relational door is opening or closing. The two of you are growing closer or more distant. Like it or not, the marital entropy that you don't want—the cooling, the closing, the distancing—will happen automatically. But the intimacy you *do* want is well worth the ongoing effort required to secure and maintain it.

This caution applies to *all* the seasons of your marriage, but the first few years are a particularly hazardous time.

Dealing with the dailies

In chapter 1 we introduced the dailies—and here we acknowledge that some couples choose cohabitation prior to marriage and thus may have established their daily routines before the wedding. For many reasons—indeed, too many to cover in this book—we strongly discourage cohabitation. Couples who are considering moving in together prior to marriage should read *Before You Live Together* by David Gudgel (Regal Books, 2003) before they take this particular plunge.

The everyday routines of married life have to be done whether you abide in a palace or a one-room apartment. Living space needs to be procured and set up. Each person's stuff needs to be sorted out and put away. Food has to be bought and prepared. Wake-up, bathroom, and bedtime routines need to be established. Work schedules need to be coordinated. The place needs to be cleaned. Clothes need to be washed and put away. Trash needs to be taken out. The yard needs to be tended. One or more cars need to be kept running. Bills need to be paid.

Most of these details probably weren't a regular part of the dating and courtship activities, and they're definitely not as much fun as dinner and a movie. Speaking of which, the availability of funds, or lack thereof, to pay for date nights out and other niceties—or simply to cover the rent—is an issue that must be navigated. During the first several months of marriage, a couple must come to grips with (a) how much they make, and (b) how much they need to make ends meet, with or without a cushion for fun stuff. *This is a critical time to talk out and establish sound financial habits.*

We'll readily confess that for far too long we believed that any money issues in our home could be solved by making more money. During our first three years of marriage, we lived on Paul's not-exactly-whopping family practice residency salary, and when he graduated to private practice, his income more than doubled. Given the paltry sum that residents took home every month in the mid-1970s, that increase wasn't exactly a fortune, but it provided a little breathing room . . . for a while. Within a few years Paul's paycheck doubled again. That was nice—until we bought our first home and then soon after were asked to buy into the practice Paul had joined. Money became tight again. What to do? Of course—get on a game show! (We were actually in a small group in which every couple, including us, had a game show windfall during the same year.) Oops, that money didn't last. Now what? I know, join a popular multilevel marketing business that seemed to be a rite of passage for young couples back then. Oh no! Selling stuff and recruiting other people to sell stuff is harder than it sounds. Better start seeing more patients every day. (Anything but restrain the spending.) And so it went.

Here's a hot tip that we can verify from firsthand experience: *If you don't learn self-discipline with spending early in the game, making more money simply allows you to get into much more financial trouble than when you made less money.* Why? Because you feel as if you can buy things, you can acquire a wallet full of credit cards, and you can usually secure loans to buy *big* things—without counting all of the costs. Trust us, the bills all come home to roost sooner or later.

Establishing a new civilization

One important activity for newly married couples, as we described in chapter 4, is to create a new civilization. Intentionally establishing that new civilization requires incorporating manners and customs of the bride's and groom's families and incorporating many others that are new and unique to the United States of You and You. (This includes setting up policies and boundaries with in-laws.) What can easily trip up newlyweds is that each person had different ways of doing the various dailies before marriage, and adjustments are going to be necessary. For example, a common sticking point is the fact that one person is usually more fastidious about cleanliness and order than the other. Whose level of order or disorder will prevail? Who will be responsible for dealing with dishes and dirty clothes? Perhaps the groom's mom took care of these chores at his home, but the bride doesn't want to assume the role of solo housekeeper. Who will take care of things that break or malfunction around the new living quarters? Perhaps the bride's father was Mr. Fix-it, and the groom doesn't know one end of a hammer from the other.

If these and a million other details aren't talked through—hopefully using good communication tools that you read about in chapter 3, right?—little annoyances will slowly accumulate into big resentments. On the other hand, if these are worked out over time with a spirit of mutual respect and a gracious recognition of each person's strengths and weaknesses, the new civilization is more likely to run more smoothly and effectively. Ideally, this process will include some positive changes on both sides. The person who was messy may acquire some grown-up habits that help maintain order (and the other person's sanity). If one has been an obsessive neat freak, the other may help him or her lighten up a little—an important survival skill if and when infants and toddlers enter the picture. Here's an example of a composite couple who had to deal with a common financial scenario that can seriously impact the forging of a new civilization:

Like many couples caught in the 2008 economic downturn, Stan and Grace faced a tough decision halfway through the first year of their marriage. Stan was an architect whose work was drying up, and his paycheck followed suit. At the same time, Grace's hours as a receptionist at a local clinic were suddenly cut, leaving them without enough money to pay the rent. After much discussion, they accepted an invitation from her parents to move into their home until the economy turned around.

Stan had always gotten along well with Grace's family, and her parents did their best to respect the young couple's need for privacy. But as the months wore on, Stan had a gnawing sense of irritation that he couldn't pin down. After some reflection and a few conversations with friends who were more seasoned in marital matters, he realized that he felt like a visitor to another culture rather than the codirector of his own. (Sleeping in his wife's old bedroom didn't help.) With the encouragement of their friends and the wise support of Grace's parents, he and Grace took some deliberate steps to establish their own civilization within the confines of her childhood home. This required some ingenuity and a lot of town-hall meetings with her parents around the kitchen table, but some issues have remained unresolved for Stan.

For example, Grace's family has long maintained a pack-rat mentality, keeping almost everything that has entered their lives because "we might need it someday." The stacks of stuff in every room have driven Stan crazy, and on many occasions he has fought off the impulse to park a Dumpster in front of the home and start shoveling. Even if he hasn't been able to fulfill this dream, Grace understands his need for order and is willing to shift in that direction once they are finally under their own roof again.

Changes in self-care

Unless the wife works outside the home, she may be fighting the natural tendency to neglect the self-care routine she maintained during her courting years. Also, one or more pregnancies during the early years of marriage will have profound effects on everyone (discussed in the next section), but especially on the wife's anatomy and physiology. She of course will gain weight during the pregnancy, but then she may find that those extra pounds just hang around long after the newborn stage is over. If she's providing care for one or more infants and/or toddlers, it will be difficult for her to find even the *time* for self-care, much less the motivation. Why bother when you're soon going to be covered in baby food and spit-up?

If the husband has a white-collar job, he might be paying more attention than ever to dress and grooming if he's trying to impress his superiors or clients, which unfortunately can draw a widening contrast between what he sees at work and what he sees at home. If the home front has been chilly or stormy, he may even be at risk for wandering eyeballs if any co-workers happen to be attractive. (If he has a job where dress and grooming *isn't* important, he may mimic his wife's lack of self-care.)

Although we may protest that grooming and extra weight *shouldn't* affect one's response to a spouse, Teri has repeatedly found that it can indeed have an impact on sexual dynamics—on both sides of the bed. Reasonable efforts to maintain one's appearance have another important consequence: They help build confidence and self-respect, which carry a powerful allure of their own.

Pregnancy, childbirth, and beyond—the big changer

We had been married for all of five months when Teri fainted one morning in church while singing the third verse of a hymn. (This occurred back in the primeval days when we all held hymnals.) She had always been physiologically prone to fainting, so Paul wasn't too worried. However, a sweet elderly woman behind us chirped, "I'll bet she's pregnant!" *Ha!* we thought, *not a chance*, having planned to wait a few years before starting a family. God had other plans.

To prove the elderly lady wrong, we performed a low-tech pregnancy test in the clinic where Paul served as a first-year resident in family practice. His eyeballs widened as he watched the telltale chemical reaction. *She was right!* All Paul could think at the time was *Our lives will never be the same.*

Still shell-shocked, we went to a family birthday celebration that evening. When we waited for a break in the conversation to say, "We have an announcement . . . ," about eight people shot back, "You're pregnant!" *How does everyone seem to get this information out of left field?* (Duh . . . What else would we be announcing five months after our wedding?) Then we nodded, and the group, including two grandparents-to-be, erupted with cheers and tears. We were glad *they* were happy about this.* But Paul was right—our lives would never be the same.

We gradually got used to the idea that we would no longer be just a couple, and we proceeded with checkups, prenatal classes, preparations, and baby showers. We were going for the full-on alternative natural-birthing-center delivery thing, only to have Chad delivered via C-section. Teri's epidural was performed by an anesthesiologist whom Paul had never seen before, and the new doctor looked as if he had just graduated from high school. This did not inspire Paul's confidence. The procedure didn't go all that smoothly, and Teri was uncomfortable before, during, and after the delivery. Chad, all 8 pounds 12 ounces of him, thrilled his grandparents. Paul was grossed out. Teri was in pain, and nursing was difficult for her. And we were both exhausted. *My wife will never be the same*, Paul thought.

Chad had been pretty mellow in the newborn nursery, but after we took him home, he seemed to turn into another kid, as though

---

* Teri was actually told by some co-workers at an upscale private school that it was too early in the marriage to have a child, and that she should consider terminating her pregnancy. One night 20 years later, as a large college choir was singing our son's beautiful arrangement of "Be Thou My Vision," it truly hit us how utterly insensitive, boneheaded, and evil that advice was.

someone had put fresh batteries in him. We put him in a bassinet next to our bed and then lay awake all night listening to him wiggle around, wondering when he was going to cry. That lasted only one night, and then he was relocated to a crib in an adjacent room. We had no trouble hearing him when he was hungry. Teri was still sore, nursing was still difficult, and Paul didn't like the sound of Chad's crying, which sounded accusatory, especially at three in the morning. (*You aren't doing a good job, because I'm uncomfortable and you can't figure out why.*) Paul was astounded at the amount of time and attention this tiny person seemed to require of us. *Wow, our lives are really never going to be the same,* he thought. It took him quite awhile, even with the letters MD following his name, to realize that a newborn can do squat for himself and has only one way to summon some assistance. His survival thus depends on the fact that his cry is engineered to make every adult within earshot extremely uncomfortable until whatever is needed to stop it takes place—changing, feeding, rocking, and so on.

During one particularly rough night, Teri's mom took over the attempts at baby calming when both of us had literally had it. "Well," she noted, "at least you know where he is!" (The truth of that observation would be lost on us until about 17 years had passed.) The seasoned pediatrician who took care of Chad (and who also mentored the family practice residents in Paul's program) was quite amused at his sad account of the sleepless nights with the crying newborn. The doctor knew it would instill some empathy in Paul for frazzled parents of fussy babies in future years, and he was right.

When Chad was a few months older and was ready to rise and shine before either of us wanted to get up, Paul would take him into the living room of our apartment, lie down on the couch, and try to snooze while holding a pacifier in Chad's mouth. This would work for about two minutes at a time. *We're never going to get a good night's sleep again,* Paul moaned.

When our daughter Carrie was born about two years later, Paul was amazed at how little attention she seemed to need. What does a newborn do, after all? Nurse, sleep, look around for short periods of time, pee, poop, cry until whatever she needs is handled—that's it. She wasn't any easier or harder than her older brother had been, but it didn't seem all that complicated to care for her. Chad, on the other hand, like any toddler in full-blown exploratory mode, had to be monitored constantly.

By now Paul had finished residency and joined a small family practice group. Paul was trying to do a good job taking care of patients, perpetually second-guessing his decisions. Teri had concluded that her brain had turned to mush. (Example: Carrie was asleep, Chad would wander into another room, and Teri would continue to watch *Sesame Street.*) The highlight of her day was watching the late-afternoon reruns of *The Bob Newhart Show* and *The Mary Tyler Moore Show,* and heaven help any child or adult who interfered with that one-hour break. Paul had never seen her look so weary or despondent at the end of the day.

Any of this sound familiar? If you have one or more kids already, you know that nothing changes your life and your marriage like having a child. We should quickly add that our child-rearing years weren't pure misery but rather were a fairly typical time of highs, lows, and in-betweens during which we did some things better than others. They illustrate a few take-home lessons and potential pitfalls from our (and many others') experiences.

One big take-home: *It's extremely important that children receive consistent love, attention, and (as they get to toddlerhood and beyond) guidance and molding from* both *parents; they should not, however, become the ultimate center of gravity in your marriage.* A couple at the wedding altar begins a new, unique civilization, even if they have one or more children from prior relationships. Their children enter into that civilization, are cherished in it, impact (and hopefully enrich) it, and eventually leave it. When they finally leave the nest, what you want is a deeper, richer relationship with your spouse, with both of you ready and eager to begin all kinds of new adventures. What you *don't* want is this: "Now what do I do with myself?" and "By the way, who exactly is this person with whom I've shared my bed for the past 20-odd years?"

Given the profound physical, physiological, emotional, and spiritual changes that occur during pregnancy, childbirth, and nursing, moms are particularly at risk for letting the baby become the ongoing center of the universe. Even if a wife is aware that this isn't a good idea and consciously tries to avoid it, it's all too easy for a husband to feel as if he has been put on the back burner. His wife doesn't feel or look the same during the pregnancy, and she may not feel "normal" for weeks, if not months or years, afterward. She is likely to be exhausted, for many reasons, and definitely doesn't feel sexy. Her breasts, once a source of sensual pleasure for both, are under new management. If sleeping with the baby becomes part of the living arrangements, the marriage is even more likely to be sexually challenged.

Perhaps no season of a marriage requires more intentionality for maintaining intimacy—of all types—than that of parenting infants and toddlers. Here are some practical suggestions:

1. Strive to guard the first year of your marriage as much as possible to allow time for the all-important conversations that establish your new civilization. As we said emphatically in chapter 2, be deliberate about taking time to find out how your spouse is doing. You'll need to exercise some creativity to make this happen when you have children. If this applies to you, go back to chapter 4, "Job no. 1 for newlyweds: Creating a new civilization," for a refresher.

2. Remember that checking-in conversations aren't the same as date nights, which may themselves require even more creativity if a newborn is in the house. No visiting grandparents, babysitter, or expense is needed to have a checking-in session, but instead a couple needs only to find the right time, some quiet space, and undivided attention from both parties. Some important stuff to talk about will likely surface. For example, the husband may be growing dissatisfied ("What happened to the lighthearted playfulness we used to enjoy?"), and at the same time the stay-at-home wife may become resentful ("We may have made this baby together, but I'm the one stuck here listening to him scream night and day").

If the wife works outside the home, she may develop a sense of unfairness that she is expected to shoulder more than half of the household and child-care duties. Often, even if the husband is changing his fair share of diapers, the mom is actually taking the primary responsibility for keeping a supply of diapers and other baby products at home, tracking how much the baby is eating, researching potty training, scheduling medical checkups, and so on. All too often Dad can unconsciously slip into a role of babysitter rather than a true co-parent (especially when the wife is a stay-at-home mom), leading her to an unsettling sense that the buck is always going to stop with her. These issues can lead to a drastic reduction in emotional connectivity, especially when both parents are exhausted from interrupted nights of sleep.

3. Beware of drifting into separate arenas when children are in the infant and toddler stages. Mom will usually seek out the company of other young moms for "tea and sympathy" while Dad buries himself into getting more established in his role as provider. One or both may drift toward a world the other doesn't relate to, reducing the amount of commonness between them. This can occur despite the fact that a mutually satisfying and functional routine may have been established in the civilization. *Husbands take heed:* If your wife doesn't work outside the home, she is dying for adult conversation after a day of listening to little ones. Be sure she gets regular doses from you. *Wives take heed:* You may not feel all that interested in what is going on with your husband at work or elsewhere when it's all you can do to keep your head above water, but your "I'm all ears" questions about what he's doing and thinking mean a lot to him.

Husbands, you don't have the "equipment" to nurse a baby, but that doesn't mean you have to wait until your child is ready for softball practice to show up for parenting duty. You can become a world-class diaper changer. You can bathe the baby and rock him or her to sleep. If you don't have any experience with these procedures, they're easy to learn. (By the way, wives tend to become quite enamored with husbands who lovingly care for an infant son or daughter.)

4. Check the head count in your bed. In the midst of trying to survive the "24-7-ness" of exhausting care for small children, or because of an intentional philosophy that favors having infants and small children sleep with their parents, some couples turn the marital bed into the family bed. We're not going to detour into the safety questions and precautions related to sleeping beside little ones or weigh in here on the location of a new baby's sleeping quarters. However, from the perspective of status of the bond between husband and wife, Teri has seen more than a few issues in the counseling office when sleeping with kids goes on for months and years. For a more detailed look at the question of the sleep locations for infants and small children, see Focus on the Family's *Complete Guide to Baby and Child Care*, rev. ed. (Carol Stream, IL: Tyndale House, 2007), 150–59, 178–79, 213–14, and 230–31.

While it may feel very cuddly to have a toddler snuggling into bed with Mom and Dad, this fosters an unhealthy dynamic in what is supposed to be a sacred retreat for just the executive unit of the civilization. Also, as the woman's libido is going to be at an all-time low during this phase of her life, she often may have an unconscious motivation to desexualize the marriage bed. Tucking an innocent, restless, sleep-sideways little bundle between herself and her husband provides a de facto negative answer to his increasingly desperate query, "Hey, sweetie, any chance of sex *tonight*?"

Bottom line: *Sleeping with a baby in the marriage bed should take place only if—and only as long as—both husband and wife are enthusiastic about it.* At the first sign of decreased fervor for this idea on the part of either person, get the little ones into their own beds.

"Good cop/bad cop" or a mighty fortress?

Once a couple has survived the newborn and infancy stages with one or more children, they will face a critical assignment in the immediate future. Somewhere between the first and second birthday, every child, whether easy or difficult as an infant, is going to force the Big Question: *Who's in charge here?*

This is inevitable, unavoidable, and entirely normal, and it will occur in a zillion different ways. The issue isn't *why* they do it—that's like asking why gravity exists—but rather *how well you handle it.* To do this well as a couple requires (guess what?) a number of those "I'm all ears" conversations we keep talking about.

If you want to get an idea of how badly things can go wrong with establishing parental control, watch any episode of *Supernanny*. Nearly every episode is a variation on the same plotline: We see a family situation in which one or more kids are *way* out of control. Blatant disobedience, utter chaos, hitting, yelling, and tantrums exhaust and exasperate the parents, who are ready to resign from the job. They call Supernanny (aka Jo Frost) for help, and she arrives in a big black London taxicab. She assesses the situation, amusingly aghast at how crazy things are in the home, and works with the parents to restore order. Whatever else is going on, inevitably a moment of truth arrives in which she insists that the parents *get on the same page and take charge of their children.*

Why is this so hard for most parents? Because attitudes about rearing kids (just like attitudes about sex, money, and other primal issues) are powerfully affected by each person's family of origin and self-concept—the stuff we talked about earlier in this book. Were your parents strict disciplinarians, highly permissive, or a mix of both? You may follow their example or go the opposite direction if you didn't like how their approach worked. Do you have a strong self-concept or desperately feel the need for approval most of the time? This will affect your willingness to make your children temporarily unhappy as a consequence of their misbehavior.

These basic inclinations about raising children can strain a relationship when two people have differing ideas about where boundaries should be drawn. If no conscious understanding and compromise exist between the two sets of assumptions (which involve, of course, a lot of respectful talking and listening), a couple will tend to start playing "good cop/bad cop" with their young children. In so doing they will unknowingly push the other person to an extreme version of whatever position he or she started with. For example, the one who draws a harder line on discipline will feel compelled to be *more* strict to compensate for the other's "lax" approach, and vice versa. (In chapter 3 we presented a detailed example of this scenario and a way to work through it. See pages 55–59 about Rob and Ellen if you need a refresher.) This, of course, leads to disrespect, feelings of frustration, and finally, distance in the marital relationship. And worse, if a unified parental front is lacking, children have an uncanny ability to manipulate situations to their advantage by working whichever parent they think will give them the answer they want at that moment.

What if you've missed some hurdles?

If you're still in this early season of your marriage and feel as though you've dropped the ball in a number of these areas, there's no time like the present to dust yourselves off and get to work. Specifically:

1. *To get a fresh start, you may need to make some heartfelt apologies to your spouse.* Acknowledging your role in any glitches that have occurred thus far will go a long way toward productive conversations.

2. *Speaking of which, make sure that your communication skill set is moving you in the right direction.* If conversations regularly involve eye rolling, snorting, voice raising, door slamming, and the like, *get some help immediately* from a counselor or a mentor couple.

3. *Start or reinstitute checking in and date nights.*

4. *Take an honest look at the assumptions (usually from your family of origin) and anxieties that each of you has brought to the marriage.*

5. *Above all, make sure that your marriage takes its rightful place in your priority hierarchy.* This may mean making some tough decisions about work hours, extracurricular activities, time spent with in-laws, kids in your bed, and so forth.

If you're 10 or 20 years down the marital road, you may be groaning as you read this chapter. *Wow, we really got off to a rocky start.* Nevertheless, you can grow closer by processing what happened, understanding the assumptions each of you brought into the marriage, and hopefully adopting a kinder and more generous posture toward your spouse.

Exercise: Stage coaching (years 0 through 5)

If you're currently in this stage of marriage, answer these questions in a journal. Then pick a few to ask your spouse during check-in time.

1. When you married, did you really comprehend that at some point the euphoria of the honeymoon would end and the relationship would actually take disciplined effort to maintain?

2. Do you think you and your spouse have successfully established your separate civilization (apart from your families of origin)?

3. What major "bumps in the road" did you hit during the first
   few years of marriage? How successful were you and your
   spouse in resolving the disagreements? ("Resolving" meaning
   each felt heard by the other, forgiveness was asked for and
   given, and a compromised solution was agreed upon.)

4. On a scale of 1 to 10 (10 being the best), how would you rate
   your physical self-care routine since marrying? How would
   you rate your spouse's?

5. If children have been added to your new civilization, how
   well do you think you and your spouse have done in maintaining your sense of "couplehood" now that your energies are
   diverted toward parenting?

6. If you have children, do any of them sleep in bed with you on
   a regular basis? If they do, does this hinder your intimacy
   with your spouse?

7. If you have children, is there any tension over child-rearing
   practices between you and your spouse?

8. What would it take to get you and your spouse back to how
   you felt toward each other right after the honeymoon?

If this stage of marriage is behind you . . .

1. How would you have answered the previous questions when
   you were in this stage of marriage?

2. What three things do you wish you could go back and redo
   during this stage?

If you are not married yet . . . look at the previous list of questions,
and decide which one seems the most daunting. What plans can you
make to ensure that your first years of marriage go more smoothly than
you would expect?

8

Under the Radar: Years 6 Through 20

> We live our lives as if we're on freight trains
> that are rumbling through town. We don't
> control the speed—or at least we think
> we don't—so our only option is to get off.
> Stepping from the train and taking life more
> slowly is very difficult.
>
> –Dr. James Dobson, *Bringing Up Boys*

In the mid-1990s Paul spent nearly three years serving as the primary author of Focus on the Family's *Complete Book of Baby and Child Care*, which offered comprehensive advice for parenting kids from prebirth through the teen years. A striking feature of that project was that several chapters were required to cover infancy through the preschool years, several more for the adolescent years, and only one for the years 5 through 11. In that chapter we asked,

Doesn't anything happen between preschool and junior high?

Actually, plenty is going on: physical growth, maturing emotions,

the acquisition of a host of intellectual and physical skills, the shap-
ing of moral values, and yes, the gradual approach to that eventful
transition to adulthood known as adolescence. All of these changes
are important and need plenty of parental guidance, prayer, and
input. This is not time for Mom and Dad to put their parenting
skills on autopilot as their child cruises through the elementary
grades.[1]

Similarly, married couples during this season, roughly the 6- to 20-
year stretch, are at risk of going on autopilot for several predictable reasons. Typically at this point in their marriage, husband and wife have
established their civilization, one way or another. (This may have been
a healthy and intentional process or merely one of settling into a routine by default.) One or both partners are digging into a career, or at
least a steady job. If they've lived in one place for any length of time,
they've probably built some connections with friends, community, and
church. Additionally, if they have their heads screwed on reasonably
straight, it's also likely that they've been tapped for some leadership
roles in these settings.

If children have been added to the family, they are typically entering the preschool or elementary school years during this season, which
means that family life will move to the rhythm of predictable calendars built around class and vacation schedules. And that's just the beginning. If kids become involved in sports, church groups, Scouts, music,
dance, performing arts, or other activities, these won't happen without
meetings, practices, rehearsals, games, and performances. Parents may
start to feel like taxi drivers shuttling kids around to these various com-

mitments—and that doesn't include whatever the kids want to do with their friends just for fun.

For many couples these are stable, satisfying, busy, and enjoyable years. The kids have shed their diapers and their toddler tantrums. You can all go to a movie, a campout, or a ball game together. You can take your children to the museum or a national park. They have yet to enter the adolescent years and all of the associated changes and (at some point) drama that accompany them. If there are grandparents in the picture, they're still likely to be mobile and highly engaged with their grandchildren. In fact, they may have the resources to take your children (and you, too, if you're nice) on some outings you can't afford.

So what can go wrong with this picture? Sadly, in the course of leading the good life, you can easily lose track of what's going on under the radar in your spouse's mind and heart. Even if you've established an amicable and cooperative system for running your civilization, it's all too easy (and common) to stop making deposits into the marital intimacy account. Without realizing it, you may be sowing the seeds of unfamiliarity that will grow and bear their toxic fruit especially after children grow up and leave the nest.

Here are some specific trouble spots:

1. Lack of margin (aka routine panic). You read about it in chapter 4, and this is the stage of a marriage where a marginless lifestyle is most likely to rear its panting, ugly head. The husband may be in a feverish career track pursuing a brass ring, not yet having realized that at the end of the day (and his life), only his relationships with God and those he loves matter—and that the rest is destined to become landfill. If the wife is working outside the home, she may be struggling to be a supermom—the high-energy action heroine who looks fabulous, has a fabulous career, is a fabulous parent, has a fabulous home, and is a fabulous lover to her fabulous husband. Supermom, of course, is a figment of the collective imaginations of the advertising and entertainment media. She provokes normal earthbound women into overwrought efforts to imitate her, or to feel like failures when they realize they can't. (A woman's realization that she cannot have it all may also generate some resentment over what feels like the unfairness of biology. Not only does her husband seem to pay a lesser price for the privilege of parenthood, but he may be unable to comprehend how she feels about it.) Add to this mix a complicated calendar of children's activities, and there is likely to be too little time or energy remaining at the end of the day for spouses to perform the checking in that's required for a proper update and reknitting of souls. And that's on a good day.

2. *Disconnects between the workforce and the home front.* Whether or not a wife works outside the home, there can be a growing disconnect between her daily experiences and those of her husband. Asking probing questions at the end of a mutually exhausting day may not be on either person's front burner:

"How was work?"

"Fine. How was your day?"

"Fine."

End of discussion.

In addition, each person is likely to develop separate spheres of friendships. Women make friends with other mothers of school-age children, and either working partner makes friends at work. This isn't in itself harmful, but it adds to diverging paths of experiences and outside influences.

One evening we were sitting at a long table in a banquet room, having dinner with several couples who were involved in a nonprofit group we support. Paul, on Teri's right, was talking with a couple across the table, while Teri struck up a conversation with the man seated to her left. She didn't know him very well and began asking questions about his occupation, which was somewhat technical and complicated to explain. As a learning exercise Teri shifted into counselor gear and asked him a series of "tell me more" questions. He became quite engaged in this process, and after a while his wife, sitting on his left, began to lean over and listen in. "Wow," she finally said to Teri, "in the last 20 minutes you've heard more about what he does than I've gotten from him in the past 10 years."

Oops. The problem wasn't that Teri was flirting or that this man's marriage was on the rocks. It was simply a question of one person "dialing in," showing interest, paying attention to the other.

3. More good cop/bad cop? In the previous chapter we described the perils of divergent child-rearing approaches. If you weren't aligned in your parenting protocols but managed to survive the toddler and preschool years, you may be lulled into a false sense that all is well during the elementary-school and preadolescent years, especially if you aren't dealing with direct challenges to your authority. The bad news is that your kids will be working overtime to develop their divide-and-conquer skills, which will be finely honed by the teen years. These will only drive a wide wedge between husband and wife if they aren't dealt with decisively.

If you're not on the same parenting page as your spouse and you have one or more children in this age group who *are* openly defiant, God help you (and we mean that literally). You'll have your work cut out for you. For one thing, with a toddler or preschooler you have the advantage of physical strength, if needed, to enforce a time-out or other consequence of misbehavior. That won't be possible (nor would it be a desirable tactic) with an older child. But even worse is the prospect of managing one eruption after another when Mom and Dad don't agree on the proper course of action. Not only will there be an abundance of conflict with their offspring, but the parents' energy will be diverted and sapped by their own arguments over the appropriate response to their child's ongoing insurrection. You can also count on plenty of shaming and blaming to boot ("It's your fault that Colin is so out of control . . ."), and fair odds that the marriage won't survive a protracted disturbance of this type.

4. Taking your eyes off the (developmental) ball. As children begin to emerge into adolescence, there should be a shift in their bond from Mom to Dad, *especially* for any of the boys in the family. If Dad hasn't been sufficiently available prior to adolescence, things can get dicey at this point. He may not know how to relate to the tweens and younger teenagers, and Mom in turn can become increasingly frustrated. At some level she'll sense her waning influence over her male child(ren) and resent the fact that Dad isn't stepping up to the plate to take over.

In addition, though female children stay bonded to Mom as their role model, the importance of Dad's role with early teenage daughters cannot be underestimated, especially for modeling the kind of treatment that should be expected from males. Also, the stage when a girl is 13 to 14 years old can sometimes put incredible strain on the mother-daughter bond, at which point a strong father-daughter bond can help keep the family from going off the rails. So if Dad doesn't step up during this parenting phase, Mom may feel that an unfair burden has been laid on her, and a huge rift can develop in the marital relationship.

Unfortunately, the timing of this stage usually coincides with the busiest time in Dad's career arc, and it's all too easy for him to become inattentive to the home front, especially when Mom seems to have managed so nicely during the children's single-digit years.

5. Adios libido. In the daily swirl of dealing with children's homework, playdates, lessons, and practices, a woman may find that her libido is going AWOL (if it hasn't already), especially if she no longer desires to become pregnant. That will only worsen if she's constantly on the go and is thoroughly exhausted by the end of the day. As we mentioned in chapter 5, the wife is mystified as to where her interest in sex went and is too tired to go hunting for it. The husband feels resentful that the most gratifying expression of love from his wife has all but disappeared.

On top of that, romantic getaways are typically replaced by family vacations. If husband and wife rightly understand that the childhood meter is running and the kids will only be home for a season, they'll want to make the most of the time they have with them. Ideally, these times are centerpieces of enjoyment and bonding between generations. (They can be the opposite as well, but that's another story.) There are also likely to be limits on time and money, not to mention the complicated logistics of child care if Mom and Dad want to get away by themselves. As a result, opportunities for an unhurried emotional and physical encounter at a secluded rendezvous become increasingly scarce, and rarely seized.

6. *The whatever-year itch.* In 1952 playwright George Axelrod appropriated the term *seven-year itch* as the title and subject of a play, followed by a 1955 film, in which a character flirted with infidelity. The phrase has remained in the cultural vocabulary since that time, suggesting a risk for relational turbulence after seven years of marriage. No curses relate to a specific anniversary; however, after a few years of getting a good hard look at a spouse's strengths and weaknesses, perhaps punctuated by the demands of bearing children and caring for them, some degree of disillusionment is inevitable. *This is a critical passage for every marriage,* and we'll look at it in more depth in chapter 10.

Needless to say, disillusionment may focus on the spouse (*Wow, Mike really has a thing about getting his way*) or married and parental life in general (*I'm not sure this is what I signed up for*), or even both. This season can be particularly dangerous for the wife, who may be wondering if she's still attractive after enduring a couple of pregnancies. Even if her libido has been dormant at home, it can be stirred in the wrong direction by a need to attract male attention in response to the nagging question, "Am I still sexy?"

The great commandment for this season

In *The Life You've Always Wanted,* a highly engaging book on spiritual disciplines, pastor and author John Ortberg tells the following story:

> Not long after moving to Chicago, I called a wise friend to ask for some spiritual direction. I described the pace at which things tend to move in my current setting. I told him about the rhythms of

our family life and about the present condition of my heart, as best
I could discern it. What did I need to do, I asked him, to be spiritually healthy?

Long pause.

"*You must ruthlessly eliminate hurry from your life,*" he said at
last. Another long pause.

"Okay, I've written that one down," I told him, a little impa-
tiently. "That's a good one. Now what else is there?"

. . . Another long pause.

"There is nothing else," he said.

He is the wisest spiritual mentor I have ever known.[2]

Of all the advice we could offer for this season of your marriage,
none seems more fitting than this. *You must ruthlessly eliminate hurry
from your life, your marriage, and your time with your children.* The reason you must be ruthless is that hurry, the great sickness of developed
countries in modern times, will insinuate itself into your life at every
turn, but especially during these particular years.

Ortberg goes on to say that

hurry is the great enemy of spiritual life in our day. Hurry can
destroy our souls. Hurry can keep us from living well. As Carl
Jung wrote, "Hurry is not *of* the devil; hurry *is* the devil."[3]

Hurry is also the great enemy of intimacy in marriage, of knowing
and being known, of keeping up with who your spouse is becoming.
If you're entering this season of marriage or are already well into it and

finding yourself going pedal to the metal most of the time, back up and reread the section "Key question no. 7" in chapter 4 that deals with creating margin in your life. In addition, think about the following:

1. *Pick and choose carefully the number of ongoing commitments you make.* Remember that it's always much easier to say no before you get involved in something rather than when you're neck deep in responsibilities.

2. *Pick and choose carefully the number of ongoing commitments your kids make.* A good rule of thumb to consider is limiting nonschool activities (sports, dance, etc.) to one per child. It should go without saying that both parents should sign off on the scheduling ramifications of any activity (not to mention how it might mesh with your family's existing commitments) before plunging into something new.

3. *Think outside your roles.* It's all too easy to start thinking of your mate in terms of the various functions he or she carries out as part of the daily or weekly routine. A wise couple will intentionally devise ways to vary the roles they play in the family and change the routine itself from time to time. Doing so requires some ongoing conversation about what's working (and what isn't).

4. *Guard the five things that are inevitably compromised when the schedule gets intense.* These activities maintain your health and sanity, as well as the relationships that matter most. They can easily disappear from your life unless they become habits you maintain automatically, month in and month out. Often they must be carved out of a frantic schedule by making actual entries in your calendar, appointments you take as seriously as any meeting. This won't be easy, and you can count on numerous false starts and flops along the way. But even modest gains in these five areas will make a huge difference in your marriage:

- *Sleep.* Human beings, including you, need at least seven hours of sleep every night. Eight is better, but you probably consider this amount an indulgence for a holiday weekend rather than part of your normal routine. Think again. Paul sees a lot of people who struggle with chronic fatigue and irritability, which (among many other things) erode joy and intimacy in marriage. Often an increase in the quantity and quality of sleep makes a decisive difference.

- *Exercise.* A half-hour walk five days per week is a starting place. Strengthening and stretching exercises twice a week (after proper training) are the next step. The health benefits of regular exercise are far too numerous to list here, but in addition to being healthy, exercise can help maintain your visual appeal to your mate. Exercising together can also be a great way to get caught up on current events. (We frequently use walks for this purpose.)

- *Choosing and preparing healthy food (and enjoying it together).* This takes time, while the fast-food drive-through or the pizza delivery doesn't. Guess which of these is associated with weight gain and other unsavory health consequences that don't enhance your marriage? In addition, sharing an unhurried meal with spouse and children can be a regular occasion for catching up, communicating, sharing joys and sorrows, having teachable moments, and hopefully enjoying some uninhibited laughter. Deep emotional bonds can be formed at the dinner table, but you have to be intentional about creating a sacred space for family meals in your weekly schedule.

- *Meaningful, unhurried conversations with your spouse and children.* These include everything from those all-important checking-in sessions you read about in chapter 2 (and are now doing regularly, right?) to romantic getaways to those unexpected seize-the-moment times, such as a meaning-of-life question posed by a child when you least expect it. (The latter often happens as you're tucking them into bed.) By the way, making the most of these opportunities requires not only being in the same room but *fully present* as well—not distracted by the next three entries on your calendar or the five projects that are behind schedule and out of control. It takes some practice and discipline to remain focused on the person in front of you and what he or she is saying, instead of whatever you think you *should* be doing at that particular moment.

- *Time to think, journal, and pray.* You might think of these occasions as your checking-in sessions with yourself and God. Do you make time to process what is going on in your head and heart and to interact with God? Busyness can easily put your mind on autopilot, and it's critical that you make the effort to articulate your inner workings.* Otherwise you (and your spouse) may be blindsided when whatever has been percolating below the surface suddenly bursts forth.

---

* For a recent anniversary gift, Paul presented Teri with the first installment of *The Journal of What I'm Thinking About at the Moment,* with a written promise (gulp!) to add an entry every Sunday for the rest of his life. This commitment has actually worked, unlike prior random stabs at journaling that were always derailed by other pressing matters.

Exercise: Stage coaching (years 6 through 20)

If you're currently in this stage of marriage, answer these questions in a journal. During check-in time, ask your spouse to answer one or two questions.

1. On a scale of 1 to 10 (10 being the best), how would you rate your overall satisfaction with the family's weekly routine? What would have to change for you to give it a higher rating?

2. Which comes closest to describing your family's functioning most of the time: "busy but manageable" or "routine panic"?

3. On a scale of 1 to 10 (10 being the highest), how well do you feel you understand what your spouse's day is really like? Using the same scale, how well do you think your spouse understands what *your* day is really like?

4. How aligned are you and your spouse right now on child-rearing philosophies and policies? What parenting issue is causing the most stress on the marriage at this point? If you have children age 12 or older, has Dad taken a more active role in parenting?

5. On a scale of 1 to 10 (10 being the best), how satisfied are you with your sex life overall?

6. How much sleep do you average a night?

7. How many exercise sessions do you average a week?

8. On a scale of 1 to 10 (10 being the best), how would you rate your nutrition?

9. When was the last time you had an unhurried conversation with your spouse? Each child?

If this stage of marriage is behind you . . .

1. How would you have answered each of the above questions when you were in this stage of marriage?
2. What three things do you most wish you could go back and redo during this stage?

If this stage of marriage is ahead of you . . . look at the previous list of questions, and decide which one seems the most daunting. What plans can you make to ensure these years go more smoothly than you would expect?

Endnotes

1. Paul C. Reisser, *Complete Guide to Baby and Child Care*, rev. ed. (Carol Stream, IL: Tyndale House, 2007), 343.
2. John Ortberg, *The Life You've Always Wanted: Spiritual Disciplines for Ordinary People* (Grand Rapids: Zondervan, 2002), 76–77. If you don't have this book, get it immediately. You might as well buy a few extra copies to give to your friends.
3. Ibid., 77.

9

Reevaluations: Years 21 and Beyond

> We live immersed in narrative, recounting and reassessing the meaning of our past actions, anticipating the outcome of our future projects, situating ourselves at the intersection of several stories not yet completed.
>
> —Peter Brooks, professor of Comparative Literature at Yale and Princeton universities, in *Reading for the Plot*

> A successful marriage requires falling in love many times, always with the same person.
>
> —Mignon McLaughlin, 20th-century American journalist and author

In 1965 Canadian psychologist Elliott Jaques introduced the term *midlife crisis* in an article published in the *International Journal of Psychoanalysis*. This journal wasn't exactly *Reader's Digest*, but by the end of the 1970s, the concept had worked its way deeply into the cultural mainstream—often represented by comic images of guys in their 40s and 50s, with shirts unbuttoned to the navel and gold bling bling dangling over graying chest hairs, leaning against a sporty red convertible whose primary accessory was a sportier (and much younger) playmate in the passenger seat.* Although only 10–15 percent of adults are thought to experience a full-blown midlife crisis, some very real and predictable transitions and reassessments are inevitable during the 40s and 50s, the midpoint of our adult lives.

As one realizes that there are just as many miles in the rearview mirror as there are down the road, some soul-searching questions begin to provoke a relentless demand for answers: *What is the meaning of life? What is the meaning of my life, in particular? What kind of grade do I get for what I've done with the past two (or three) decades? Did I succeed or fail? Was I even going after the right thing, or have I utterly wasted 20 (or more) years of my life? Is there time for a "do over"? What do I really want to do with the second half of my life? How much am I willing to change in my present life to achieve that goal?* These questions often arise at the 20- to 25-year mark in a marriage, and they typically revolve around whatever has been the basis of each person's identity. For the husband, usually this is job performance and his track record as financial provider for the family. For the wife, identity is usually based on how well the primary relationships in her life have fared.

Indeed, there is such a profound (though predictable) list of tran-

---

* The 1980 comedy *Middle Age Crazy* represented one notable attempt by Hollywood to cash in on the midlife-crisis issue. The film was unnecessarily raunchy, although it did manage to depict the folly of marital infidelity. When a straying husband's no-strings-attached affair with a Dallas Cowboy cheerleader goes sour and he realizes that his marital commitment really matters, he offers a sad observation: "No strings—no people."

sitions converging at this juncture of a marriage that it almost seems miraculous when an unprepared couple negotiates them with the relationship intact (let alone thriving) on the other side. Because of the individual upheavals experienced by both husband and wife, major changes can rapidly occur in a civilization that has been unwavering in its routine for years. The marriage that always seemed almost boring in its predictability may, seemingly overnight, become nearly unrecognizable.

The exit of the children

The graduation of the last child from high school brings several issues to the forefront. *Did we do okay as parents? Did the kids turn out all right? Did we pass the baton of our values to them? Have we instilled enough in them to trust they can make it the rest of the way in their lives?*

The exit of kids also means an entirely new routine in the household. The home is quiet. The bathroom stays clean much longer. Trips to the grocery store become less frequent. Schedules are no longer built around games, recitals, and the need to supervise teens gathered under your roof. There are many more blank spaces on the calendar as the responsibility for supervising and ferrying and worrying about kids is drastically dialed back. Suddenly the two people who are left in the house find that the routine governing the daily flow of life for so long has abruptly changed.

If either or both parents have been overly enmeshed in the kids' lives as a way of finding emotional intimacy that wasn't available in the marital bond, things can get awkward, or even highly uncomfortable, at this point. Two people who have slept together for 25 years suddenly look across the quiet, empty house and think, *I don't really know who this person is, I don't know how to be with this person, and furthermore, I don't know if I even want to be with this person.* The necessary busyness that goes along with raising kids can be an effective delay tactic for answering the tough question, "What happened to our marriage?"

Beware: *If the marriage has been tepid or turbulent for many years, the departure of the youngest child may serve as an important trigger for the spouse who has been thinking about leaving the marriage.* Indeed, a plan to bail out at this juncture may have been secretly in the works for some time, and when it's announced, the unsuspecting spouse will be in for a grim surprise.

On the wife's side of the bed . . .

As the youngest child is launched (or at least old enough to allow for an easing of maternal vigilance), it will dawn on the traditional stay-at-home wife that she has decades ahead of her that won't involve caring for her children. If she's unprepared for this realization, an identity crisis of sorts may ensue. For the woman who has primarily invested her life in child rearing, the transition from that demanding full-time role and its wide-ranging tasks (chauffeur/cook/class mom) to a markedly condensed domestic job description can be exhilarating, utterly depressing, and everything in between. The arrival of menopause further reinforces to a woman that her identity as childbearer is irrevocably gone. Even when a woman is under no delusions that she would want to become pregnant once again at age 47, the ability to reproduce remains a core element of her identity, and its loss, for whatever reason, is keenly felt.

When a woman has spent two decades packing school lunches and running the family taxi all day, it's easy for her memories of life before kids to have long faded into the mists of time. Suddenly the last child has a driver's license, buys his own lunch, and does his own homework, so many of Mom's previous time commitments thus become virtually obsolete. If her sense of worthiness has been primarily based on relational intimacy and met in her role as Mom rather than in collaborating and cultivating soul-to-soul intimacy with her husband, this forced early retirement can be a bewildering experience. It can be particularly unsettling if she hasn't been thinking about what she's going to do with the second half of her adult life. A woman who has been working outside the home all along has probably still been the primary caretaker—that if, the one who assumes the major burden of responsibility for managing the details of the children's lives. Even if she changes nothing in her outside employment, she will still go through a time of upheaval when her daily role as "Mom" is redefined.

On the other hand, if she has developed a healthy self-concept as a competent adult, this period of newfound freedom can unleash an incredible flood of creative energy, especially if there isn't a frozen vacuum where a healthy marital bond should exist. Once the initial disorientation has passed, she begins to realize that she can dust off the dreams that may have been set aside when her children arrived. She now has the opportunity to remake herself and to proceed with the projects she never had time for. Whether she changes careers, returns to the workforce for the first time in years, enrolls in classes, takes up a new or long-abandoned hobby, volunteers to help at a local nonprofit organization, or begins cleaning out every nook and cranny of her home—including *(gasp!)* the dreaded garage—her focus is surely going to be different than it was before.

With a newfound focus on what *she* would like to do after all the years of sacrifice, the wife may become a little more selfish in asserting her own needs. A husband who has always assumed a certain eternal quality about his wife's role in the home can perceive this as threatening. In addition, as we'll see momentarily, he may finally be ready for more relational intimacy—only now to feel confused and rejected. At the very time when he may need his wife's emotional support and understanding more than he has in years, she may be feeling as if it's finally her turn to think about how *she* wants to spend her days and weeks, and the rest of her life. Also, if she decides to return to a long-delayed academic career, the costs associated with her education may put stress on the family's finances at a time when the other demands are at their peak. (The kids' departure from home often routinely coincides with a sudden spike in their expenses—for tuition, housing, a vehicle, insurance, and so on. We might refer to this postadolescent, young-adult period as the "I am so over you guys, but of course you'll pay for _____ as always, right?" years.)

On the husband's side of the bed . . .

While the tectonic plates are shifting in the wife's world, her husband begins undergoing some pretty serious seismic activity of his own. Either partner who has been working full-time outside the home will begin to wonder, *Wow . . . am I going to be able to do this job for* another *25 years?* But this question usually hits much harder for the man, because the male identity is often intricately tied to his role as provider. By this time in his career arc, he has either reached his earlier vocational goals or he hasn't. Either way, he probably doesn't have the same passion and focus for the job that he once had.

Men and women frequently experience a strange crossover at this midlife period. While the wife has previously placed the highest value on family relationships, she may now attach an equal importance to developing interests that extend outside the family. On the other hand, the husband, who has previously placed the highest value on succeeding in the workplace, may now find himself longing for deeper relationships—perhaps for the first time in his life. He may make some overtures in this direction, or he may not be able to put his desire into words. The entire notion still may be too vague, or he may never have learned a language for expressing how he feels. Either way, this can lead to utter confusion for a wife who may have deeply desired more closeness in the marriage for decades, and then has finally learned how to live *without* that kind of emotional intimacy. After years in that mode she can be quite resistant to her husband's attempts to reach out—leaving him befuddled (once again) over the complexities of the female mind.

If the husband's reevaluation leads him to conclude that his career so far hasn't been what it was cracked up to be (or perhaps it's making *him* feel as if he's cracking up), and his newfound need for relationship goes unfulfilled, he may begin to experience a deepening depression—perhaps for the first time in his life. He may resonate with King Solomon's lament in the book of Ecclesiastes, that all of his impassioned career pursuits turned out to be "vanity, a chasing after wind," while at the same time facing a growing, gnawing realization that he shortchanged his family as well. In an attempt to dampen the pain of this grim double bind, he may self-medicate with alcohol, expensive shiny toys, or other kinds of addictions. Or he may yield to the impulse to pursue a much younger woman in a misguided attempt to feel alive again.

Sex: The best of times, the worst of times

We've already covered this topic in detail in chapter 5, but a few reminders are in order. Please note our reference to the opening line of Charles Dickens's classic novel *A Tale of Two Cities*: "It was the best of times, it was the worst of times." For a marriage that has been built on a solid foundation where husband and wife have intentionally worked to know and be known by the other and where adjustments to each person's sexual needs have been thoughtfully made, this can be the best of times for sex. If emotional, soul-to-soul intimacy has been consistently nurtured through years of thick and thin, you may find that your closeness during sex takes on a whole new dimension that may have been missing when you were younger and sexier, and when intercourse was much more physically and hormonally driven.

If the kids are finally out of the house, you may be astonished at the freedom you feel to fool around without worrying about interruptions at highly inopportune moments. If you have the resources to get away for some weekends or longer time-outs involving beaches and balconies and unhurried conversations about what matters to you both, you may be very pleasantly surprised by what happens between the sheets.

But . . . if you and your spouse have spent two decades growing more distant, or have been carelessly wounding each other in fights about issues you can't even identify anymore, it can be the worst of times for sex. For not only have the emotional underpinnings been dismantled, but also the physical ones will often begin to deteriorate as well. For starters, although there are exceptions, in our 40s and 50s most of us aren't as visually appealing with our clothes off as we may have been two decades earlier. Menopause and its attendant discomforts (hot flashes, vaginal dryness) definitely don't rev up a woman's libido. Men start to tangle with erectile dysfunction, which can throw them off their sexual game, despite what those promising Viagra, Levitra, or Cialis ads portray. What may have been an unstoppable libido several years ago may also become a shadow of its former self, for all of the reasons we described in the chapter 5 sidebar "When the Wife Has More Libido Than Her Husband" (see page 122).

There are, of course, medical treatments that can reduce the discomforts of menopause, replenish testosterone if it's faltering, and revive erectile function. If the relationship is doing well, these can be a blessing when sexual function needs a little assistance. But if the marriage is on shaky ground, medical intervention won't necessarily improve matters. Teri has counseled women who have bemoaned a husband's enthusiastic deployment of a new prescription to relieve erectile dysfunction (*He's all hot to trot, as if we're back in our 20s again, and I'm anything but. Now what?*).

If your sex life currently falls into the worst-of-times category, it is definitely not too late to take some steps in the right direction. We would direct your attention back to the numerous recommendations in chapter 5 and remind you how much mutually satisfying sex depends on the quality of the other 99 percent of your waking hours. In addition, it isn't too late to seek assistance from a counselor who is experienced and comfortable dealing with this issue. (*A reminder for the guys:* If there are several areas of your marriage in need of repair, sex is usually the *last* thing to get fixed, not the first.)

Money: The best of times, the worst of times

Guess what? Mr. Dickens's quote also applies to your finances during this period of your marriage. One or both of you may well be in the thick of your peak earning potential during this period. Even if you've never earned a shoot-the-moon income, if you've been wise with your money—spending less than you earn, while giving, saving, and investing consistently—for a couple of decades, you may be well positioned at this point to enjoy some satisfying fruits of your labor. We're not just talking about creature comforts. You may now have the funds and time to invest in such rewarding pursuits as education (whether for your offspring or yourself), travel, and the causes you care about, both locally and on the other side of the world. Indeed, you may be able to take the opportunity to send yourself, and not merely your funds, to some faraway place that desperately needs what you have to offer.

On the other hand, if your marriage has been a nonstop episode of *Wallets Gone Wild*, you may find yourself having to pay some really ugly pipers as the years pass. Accrued debt, scrambling to pay bills, fights over too much month at the end of the money—you probably know the drill, and if you've been at it for two decades or more, it can really wear thin. If you add to this rising costs of living, a few medical surprises, and kids needing help getting through college and launched into adulthood, you may feel strapped in 10 different directions.

If this is your situation, we'd recommend that you review chapter 6, where the process of restoring financial order is laid out in some detail. Important news flash: *As with sex, it's never too late to start working on this area of your marriage.* Particularly crucial are the steps involving transparent, gracious, and forgiving dialogue about the process that got you where you are and the steps that you need to take toward a remedy. Also, remember that in the long haul, *it's more important to preserve your relationship than your stuff,* which is destined to become landfill.

When they hand you the gold watch . . .

Speaking of finances, stuff, and relationships, one of the biggest changes that a couple will experience is the proverbial hanging up of one or both sets of spurs. The transition to retirement usually brings up some predictable and often formidable issues in a marriage.

Anxiety about finances. Though it makes obvious sense to create a rational financial road map for the retirement years, it's truly amazing how many couples are unwilling to face an unavoidable question: "Will we be able to maintain our present standard of living on our retirement income?" Many can't answer an even more basic question: "What exactly *will* our retirement income be?"

Answering those questions requires the same stiff resolve that it takes to answer the same basic questions *before* retirement (i.e., "What is our current income?" and "Is it enough to maintain our standard of living?"). You need to make a fearless, reality-based assessment of the amount of money that is coming in (or going to come in after retirement) and the amount that is going out (or expected to go out after retirement), and then make whatever adjustments are necessary until outgo is never greater than income. You may recall from chapter 6 that this is called a budget, and most couples that Teri has worked with won't create and live by one for a number of reasons. If a couple has been resistant to adhering to a budget during the course of the marriage, then finances have been at best the cause of middle-of-the-night anxiety and at worst the source of great marital blame and resentment.

Teri is currently working with several couples who are experiencing major retirement-related stress. In three of these cases, the couples are in a state of high anxiety over whether there is enough money to live comfortably in the future. Yet even though harsh words are being volleyed back and forth, they haven't done the one thing that would seem to be an obvious course of action: Ask a financial planner to assess their situation and provide informed and neutral feedback about their options.

This unwillingness to get a handle on the financial situation usually occurs for the same reasons that interfered with this step earlier in the marriage: guilt about impulsive spending, the need to control (or not relinquish control, in the case of covert spending), or a general unwillingness to delay gratification. The approach of retirement and its attendant financial concerns may actually aggravate some of these patterns. With the looming of the sunset years can come a sense of "If not now, *when?*" Each partner may have a pet project that he or she is no longer willing to delay but that also requires a significant outlay of finances (for example, a major remodel of the home or the purchase of a fishing boat). What happens when one decides to plunge ahead without the other person being fully on board? Trouble, as you might imagine, but perhaps even more than would have occurred in years gone by. An "unnecessary" expenditure can be met with disapproval or even panic when income is going to be fixed and limited, especially if the one who is unhappy also views him- or herself as the "saver."*

Changes in the daily routine. If a couple has long been used to being apart during the workday, figuring out how to be together 24-7 can be a daunting task. It doesn't sound flattering to the relationship, but the fact is that most couples who have lived under the same roof for several decades (especially when the kids have been out of the home for years) develop a weekly routine that includes a lot of separateness. Two people become adjusted to "my time" and "our time." "My time" is for self-care, shopping, reading, hobbies, lunches with friends, and so on. "Our time" includes time on projects and activities that are mutually agreeable. But if "my time" suddenly disappears with a radical change of schedule, resentment can start to build over what feels like an invasion of privacy.

Personality clashes that used to be buffered by the routine of spending time away from each other may now become more difficult

---

* One day a For Sale notice appeared on the bulletin board in the doctor's dining room at the hospital where I (Paul) admit my patients. The item being sold was a shiny speedboat, and the sign included the boat's picture, specifications, and price. Below the price the seller included a helpful addendum: "Reason for sale: Divorce." Below that line, a local wag penciled in another: "Reason for divorce: Boat."

to avoid. Additionally, whether or not the wife has worked outside the house, the home is usually her domain. A woman can become increasingly irritated as her newly retired husband begins looking for things to reorganize around the homestead. He in turn may begin feeling as though he's being seen as an intruder in his own fortress.

What do I do with myself? Although some know exactly how they plan to spend their long-awaited retirement days, many are ill-prepared for what feels like an empty dance card in their hands. But when a person has worked every weekday for decades, the transition can be disorienting. Often there is a long list of to-dos and things to fix around the house that were put off during the years of child rearing and employment. Paul has heard several retired men describe how their list (and enjoying their favorite recreation) kept them busy for about six months, after which they started getting restless. They may drive their wives crazy or become depressed or even go back to work.

Big take-home here: *Retirement shouldn't be seen as a release from the salt mines to a life of loafing, or a time when productivity and goals are no longer important.* Rather, it's a wonderful opportunity to pursue any number of worthy endeavors that were out of reach when full-time work demanded so much time and energy. What might be on the agenda? The sky is literally the limit: Travel, education, ministry in a church or parachurch setting, volunteering, mentoring younger adults or adolescents—the opportunities to enhance your life, and help meet the needs in your community or around the world, are unlimited.

Where are we going to live? Another huge change that may come with retirement is relocation to new living quarters. Many couples make an intentional plan to move at retirement to a warmer place ("No more shoveling snow!"), a smaller place ("No more paying to air-condition four bedrooms!"), a place closer to the kids ("Let them take care of *us* for a change!"), or a retirement community ("Matching golf carts for us, and the kids can fend for themselves!"). A move at any time in your marriage is disruptive, but this one is usually the most traumatic because decades may have passed since the last change of address. Unless the move is to a smaller house five miles away, lifelong friends and community involvements may have to be relinquished. Also, most retirees downsize in a move at this stage, which requires combing through years of boxes full of memories, good and bad, for the last time. For some, the declutterizing process may be a time of manic and joyous release; for others, it will be a time of poignant grief and loss. Needless to say, any relocation at this time of life will be challenging and will strain the best of marriages.

As we finish writing this book, we're 58 and 60 and have just celebrated our 34th wedding anniversary. The retirement process is just ahead of us, and we're keenly aware that our observations about that phase of our marriage are based on what we've heard from our clients. Addressing our own margin issues (rather than just advising other people to do so) is a priority item for us over the next year. Okay, the next two years. We'll even give you permission to ask us how we're doing, but you'll have to wait a couple of years. We're planning on relying on the same old things that have taken us through all the rough stuff in the past: honest conversation, generous listening, and taking responsibility for our own responses to life. Maybe we'll write an updated version of this book in 10 years and let you know how we did.

Caring for aging and/or ailing parents

Just about the time the kids are (theoretically) launching from the household, aging parents who previously were vigorous, or at least self-sufficient, may begin experiencing serious health problems. This only adds to the pressures on a husband and wife who are already feeling unbalanced and stretched too thin. (Some writers have referred to couples in this situation as the "sandwich" generation, pressed between the needs of their teenage and/or young-adult children and their aging parents.)

Often the burden of caring for ailing parents falls most heavily on the wife. At a time when she is looking forward to a respite from the endless duties of motherhood, her own mother or father may need nurturing and assistance. In this odd role reversal, the adult child may experience an array of confusing emotions. If the aging parent provided adequate love and approval during childhood, the display of physical fragility (a signal of coming loss) can evoke poignant feelings of combined grief, sweetness, and even guilt when the requirements for care and attention feel burdensome.

If the aging parent did *not* provide that basic love and approval, strong feelings can complicate the routine of providing care. For instance, great resentment may arise over being called on to provide care for a parent from whom the grown child never felt loving care. Or a new hope may blossom: "Maybe *now* Mom will finally see my value and love me the way I always wanted to be loved." Whatever the emotional backdrop to the parent-child situation, caring for an ailing parent can exact an incredible price of time, money, and energy. This can wreak havoc in a marriage where in-law issues have already created turbulence, or when one or both partners already resent what feels like lack of attention from the other.

The death of the last parent is a time of imbalance, whether or not the relationship was healthy. At best, when Mom or Dad was loving and beloved, the grief is acute and the loss of the parent's presence in the family is disorienting for a while. At worst, the pain of losing all hope of winning Mom's or Dad's approval can lead to a shut-down-the-presses depression as the individual grapples with what the future will look like without that hope. The death of our parents also forces us to face our own mortality, as we've never allowed ourselves to do previously. We're next in line, and this realization may generate a lot of angst (*I know I'm 50 years old, but I still feel like an orphan*). It may also embolden us to make some important now-or-never changes that reflect adjustments in our values. Sentinel events like this have a way of doing that.

Spiritual reevaluations

Another major shift that can occur at this point in life is a reassessment of one's spiritual foundations. Knowing that we're on the "back nine" of life, seeing a friend or colleague struck down by an unexpected illness, walking through the death of our parents, experiencing other losses that life inevitably brings us—all of these events can raise big questions, and they should.

For someone who has quietly pushed God into the background or vigorously maintained a viewpoint that He doesn't exist, the logical conclusion—that life and death are meaningless, and the universe couldn't care less what happens to any of us—can send enough cold

chills down the spine to reopen some inner dialogue about the existence of a Creator. We would heartily encourage such dialogue and
would even propose a couple of books to fuel that process: C. S. Lewis's
classic *Mere Christianity*, and Timothy Keller's more recent but out-
standing work *The Reason for God: Belief in an Age of Skepticism* (Dut-
ton, 2008).

For someone who has spent a fair amount of time in church and
feels well versed, so to speak, in the teachings of Scripture, midlife turbulence and experiencing a few serious losses can also provoke some
rethinking of long-held assumptions. *Do I really believe what I've been
talking about all these years, or am I just repeating my church's party line
or what I learned as a kid in Sunday school? What is my faith really based
on? Have I really processed it with a grown-up mind? Do I have an understanding of God that makes sense amid the complexities of life, and a
mature relationship with Him that impacts what I do every day?*

These and others like them are great questions, and they shouldn't
be batted away as too complicated or dangerous to consider. Indeed, for
many people, addressing them will require a process of deconstructing
and reconstructing one's belief system. Reading, prayer, and some serious talks with people who won't dish out pat answers are all part of this
effort, which can and should result in a much more stable and mature
faith. (Indeed, we don't think God is particulary threatened by the
process.) It can be the basis of some great checking-in sessions that seriously enhance soul-to-soul communication with your spouse. However, it can also provoke some marital turbulence if one person is
frightened by a mate's grappling with some challenging questions:
Ohmygosh, I think John is getting ready to abandon his faith! We've been

side by side in church for all these years, and now he sounds like he's rethinking everything. Has he lost his mind?

Beware of brushing off or trying to suppress a spouse's spiritual reassessment process. Remember what we said in chapter 2 about the benefits of keeping up with what your spouse is thinking?

> If you've done a good job of listening, you have a golden opportunity to weave your own value system into what the other person is hatching. Try as you might, *you can't dictate your spouse's value system, even if you're convinced beyond a doubt that you are right.* But when you've listened without judgment or coercion, he or she will be more trusting of you, and more willing to consider your opinions and feelings.[1]

You could substitute "doctrinal stance" or "worship style" or whatever spiritual concern you might have for "value system," and this statement would still stand—with one exception. We've seen several situations in which spiritual reevaluations were actually little more than a smoke screen to justify an action that a person knew to be morally wrong. The most common of these scenarios involves the decision to walk out on a spouse, especially when there's a replacement waiting in the wings.

Spiritual rationalizations can range from "I don't think I believe that Bible stuff anymore" to "I think the Scriptures are okay with what I'm doing if my needs aren't being met" to the even more pathetic "God told me it was okay to file for divorce." A challenge to this line of thinking is definitely in order but is best put forward by good friends or a trusted pastor rather than a wounded spouse. Unfortunately, if the person has already checked out of the marriage—and especially if there's someone else in the picture—appeals to long-held articles of faith are usually dismissed as narrow-minded and judgmental.

With that exception duly noted, we heartily encourage couples to develop a habit of engaging in open and transparent conversations about their faith. These may be challenging or even a little unsettling at times, but they can also bear some rich and rewarding fruit if undertaken with a spirit of honesty, humility, and a sincere desire to deepen your relationship with your spouse and with the God who created both of you.

The path taken

This time of reevaluation often leads to a fork in the road. The reassessments that all of us experience during midlife, whether provoking minor course corrections or major upheavals, might lead you to raise a critical question about your spouse: "Is the person in my bed a total stranger, my most deeply trusted ally, or somewhere in between? Do I need to protect myself, or can I trust this person with what is brewing inside of me?"

Destructive choices are a distinct possibility when a person goes through a midlife transition alone (or worse, with the "help" of someone who is contributing an opinion out of selfish motivation). But midlife reassessments can also usher in an era of incredible freedom and renewed energy when two people who have already invested 20 to 25 years of life under the same roof decide to grasp each other's hands and walk the rest of the way together.

Figuring out how to approach a spouse from whom you have felt emotionally alienated for years isn't an easy task, but it's well worth the effort when he or she chooses to be responsive to your proposal. Extending this invitation to do things differently is the subject of the next (and last) chapter of this book. We urge you *not* to take the path of least resistance: making the assumption that your spouse is incapable of hearing you anymore. Rather, take the time to think through carefully how you might approach your mate with a proposal to work collaboratively to create the safety, peace, and emotional intimacy that perhaps disappeared from the marriage years ago. In the next chapter we'll walk you through that process.

The decisions you may make during this transitional period can lead to a literal feast or famine, boom or bust, joy or heartbreak, legacy or disaster. The bad stuff happens when the reordering of priorities creates a state of agitated impulsivity in which one or both spouses make drastic changes without carefully thinking through all the options.

Over the past few years we have grieved over some spectacularly disastrous divorces that occurred among couples we knew, and whom we thought we knew better. Indeed, these cautionary tales helped fuel our motivation to write this book. Thirty-plus-year marriages were tossed aside when one spouse decided that the other couldn't possibly "do things differently," when in fact the discarded mate was more than willing and (in our opinion) quite able to take the marriage down to bedrock and rebuild intimacy and trust. At the heart of these situations was a person who had felt unheard by the spouse for many years. The turning point involved someone else with a sympathetic ear—as described in "The plot thickens . . ." in chapter 2 and in more detail in chapter 4 (see pages 33–34 and 74–77)—and a hunger deep enough to cause the straying spouse to violate long-held convictions and spurn a lifetime of shared experiences. The fallout has included months of wrenching grief on the part of the abandoned spouse, ruptured relationships with children and grandchildren, major financial losses (lawyers and dividing possessions are costly), and spiritual consequences that only God can ultimately assess. In our humble opinion, this is too great a price to pay.

On the other hand, the resolutions that come out of this season of review and assessment can lay the groundwork for enormous productivity and deep feelings of satisfaction if the couple can negotiate this time of individual renovation with mutual understanding and openness. Their home becomes an impregnable haven that reflects a unique civilization that two people have co-created. We have had the pleasure of knowing many such couples, and being in their company is indeed refreshing and rejuvenating. We invite you to add to their number and, in so doing, serve as an example to younger couples who need living evidence that "the best is yet to come."

Exercise: Stage coaching (years 21 and beyond)

If you're currently in this stage of marriage, answer these questions in a journal. During check-in time, ask your spouse to answer one or two questions.

1. If you had children and have actually managed to get them out of the house, what is the best thing about your empty nest? What is the worst thing? If the kids are 20-somethings who are still living at home, what impact (positive and/or negative) has that had on the marriage?

2. For the husband: Do you think your wife has successfully negotiated the task of figuring out what she'd like to do with the time and energy that was previously needed in her role as mom?

3. For the wife: Is your husband as energized by his career as he once was? Do you think he's having any struggles in that area of his life?

4. On a scale of 1 to 10 (10 being the best), how satisfied are you with the current level of emotional intimacy in your marriage?

5. On a scale of 1 to 10 (10 being the best), how satisfied are you with the current level of sexual intimacy in your marriage?

6. On a scale of 1 to 10 (10 being the best), how satisfied are you with the current level of the household's financial management?

7. What are your top three fears about retirement? Have you and your spouse had any discussions about what retirement will/should look like?

8. Are you and your spouse caring for an aging or ailing parent(s) at this point? If so, how has that impacted the marriage?

9. Are you or your spouse experiencing any changes in your interest in spiritual issues?

10. If you could go back in time just once, what one thing would you do differently?

11. What one thing are you most proud of as you think about your life?

If this stage of marriage is behind you . . .

1. How would you have answered each of the above questions when you were in this stage of marriage?

2. What three things do you most wish you could go back and redo during this stage?

If this stage of marriage is ahead of you . . . look at the previous list of questions, and decide which one seems the most daunting. What needs to happen *now* in your marriage to avoid some of the pitfalls you expect in the future?

Endnotes

1. From page 35 in this book, with emphasis added here.

10

Beyond Disillusionment

> Women marry men hoping they will change. Men marry women hoping they will not. So each is inevitably disappointed.
>
> —Albert Einstein, 1999 *Time* magazine Person of the Century

> The success of marriage comes not in finding the "right" person, but in the ability of both partners to adjust to the real person they inevitably realize they married.
>
> —John Fischer, author and songwriter

> No relationship in life is more vulnerable to disillusionment than marriage.
>
> —Our humble opinion (you may quote us)

We gaze from afar at a public figure whose appearance or accomplishments grab our fancy. Not uncommonly the word *idol* describes a person who is the object of rabid public affection. But even if we know better than to idolize someone, it's all too easy to *idealize* a person we admire. We assume, usually subconsciously, that the people we place on a pedestal live on a plane well above ours. They must be smarter, more talented, more self-confident, more spiritual than we are, or perhaps all of the above. If those who are objects of this admiration have any degree of self-awareness, they are quick to point out that such an assessment is well off the mark (*If only you really knew me . . .*).

Indeed, a few years in the School of Life will teach us that those whom we might idealize are going to disappoint us sooner or later—especially once we know more about them. As a little exercise in reality checking, you can no doubt name your (least) favorite example of public figures who disillusion us:

- A politician who can't deliver on his or her campaign promises—or who is caught in a bald-faced lie
- A sports champion who admits to taking performance-enhancing drugs
- A high-profile pastor who has an affair
- A pop star who has a drug problem
- A historical icon who you discover had feet of clay

The same happens closer to home when we learn about or directly experience scenarios like the following:

- A family member who has some skeletons in the closet
- A friend who betrays our trust
- A parent whose emotions are out of control
- A spouse who _____ (fill in the blank)

In fact, *disillusionment at some level is an inevitable component of any long-lasting relationship* between two people, both of whom are always flawed. We could rightly refer to this process as *dis-illusion*: giv-

ing up the illusion that someone else is perfect.* In marriage the setup
for disillusionment is particularly potent for four reasons:

1. The "love is blind" phenomenon. As we described in chapter 1, in
the heady early days of romance, the other person's flaws are minimized
or ignored, and the relationship is idealized (*We make such beeeautiful
music together . . .*).

2. Great expectations. If the romance doesn't idealize the relationship, the wedding ceremony and reception almost certainly will. If all
of those toasts and tributes are true, what could possibly go wrong?
(Can you imagine a wedding reception at which the maid of honor
holds up a glass of champagne and says, "Now, John, you need to be
aware that Julie can be really demanding . . ."?)

3. I chose *to marry this person.* None of us chooses our parents, so
if Mom or Dad proved to be a bad apple, we shouldn't shoulder any
blame. But since arranged marriages are hardly the norm in our culture,
bride and groom usually come to the altar of their own volition. Since
each has been involved in choosing the other, misgivings later on can
be particularly galling when it appears that one didn't choose wisely
(*What was I thinking?*).

4. Up close and personal. When you live with someone, guess what
you can't keep up for long? That would be the remotest appearance of per-
fection. Whatever best foot you may have put forward during courtship,
it won't stay best *or* forward during the ongoing demands of the dailies.

---

* Disillusionment with God is another story. Usually this involves poor behavior
  on the part of people who claim to represent God, having to release some unrealistic notions about God's character and interaction with us, or coping with a terrible loss that seems to make no sense.

For many couples, one person's realization that "my spouse isn't the person I married" actually involves little more than the curtain rolling back on the other person's preexistent flaws. Inevitably, new defects will appear as well, representing an actual change of some type in the spouse. (Often these are driven by the circumstances of life or even the dynamics of the marriage itself.) It's at this point that the real work begins, and true intimacy can bloom—intimacy that's devoid of illusion and fully embraces the other person, warts and all. This is the stuff of which great marriages are made, the kind of marriages that not only endure but actually improve with age. What does it take for this to occur? Nothing less than time and effort, seasoned with ample doses of honesty, humility, grace, and generosity. We'll get to that momentarily. But for now . . .

What can contribute to disillusionment?

At first glance the answer might seem to be "almost anything you can think of." But with a little reflection it should become clear that the causes for disillusionment run a gamut from minor annoyances to truly rotten behavior. Before even considering the various ways in which one person can disappoint another, we must acknowledge that every worthwhile endeavor in life requires more effort than we ever anticipate at the starting gate. This is true whether we're talking about marriage, starting a family, becoming educated, launching a career, or even planning a vacation.

Psychiatrist M. Scott Peck opened his best-selling book *The Road Less Traveled* with a now-famous simple and profound statement: "Life is difficult." Sadly, the application to marriage comes as a grim revelation to many and may elicit a gnawing sense that "this isn't what I signed up for," along with a futile search for some greener grass. (This is also one of many reasons why marriages among the young, or the immature at any age, so frequently fail.)

Beyond the basic struggles of daily life lie some common human foibles. We all have our strengths and flaws, and living in close proximity brings them into clear focus. Here are a number of arenas in which a spouse's shortcomings become readily apparent:

Appearance. When you were dating, you probably made some sort of effort to spiff yourself up before meeting your beloved. Now that process is likely to be reserved for the workplace and perhaps for a night out. But what about the rest of your time together? What does your spouse look like sprawled and snoring on the couch, with drool hanging from one corner of the mouth? How about in the morning with Bozo hair sticking out in all directions, unshaven or without makeup, sitting on the john, wearing grubby clothes? What about the weight gain that comes routinely with pregnancies and birthdays, those pounds that don't want to leave without a fight? What about the "spare tire," the receding hairline, the deflating bustline, the graying hair, the wrinkles? Is this just cause for trading in your spouse for a newer, sleeker model?

Sex. We've already dealt at length with sexual dissatisfaction in chapter 5. Needless to say, few areas of disillusionment are likely to cut as deeply as a big gap between the eager expectation and early fireworks of sex and the fluctuations of sexual experience over the long haul of a marriage.

Money. Likewise, we've looked at financial issues in chapter 6. Mistakes, miscalculations, untamed spending habits, and dissatisfaction over a couple's earning potential can lead to lots of disappointment, along with the sinking feeling that some long-cherished desires for things and experiences in this life aren't going to happen.

Pursuits of the mind. Every couple has differences in personal interests. But what if one person loves exploring, learning, and growing, and the other isn't all that curious about life and the universe? What if one of you wants to patronize the fine arts, while the other would rather veg out in front of the tube for hours on end? What if one of you wants to spend precious vacation week(s) conquering a different corner of the globe, and the other longs to decompress by sitting on the same sunny beach each year?

Spirituality. If a couple isn't spiritually aligned prior to marriage, the pressures and losses that life inevitably brings will eventually push their differences into sharper (and usually less appealing) relief. Even if a couple is truly on the same spiritual page on their wedding day, misalignment can occur later. (Remember one theme of this book: We all change in response to the events in our lives.) One person's relationship with God may become more deep and vibrant as the years pass, while the other's remains static or becomes more shallow and distant. One person may become disenchanted by a spouse's apparent legalistic focus on rules and regulations or by a tendency in the opposite direction toward an apparent *lack* of concern for behavioral boundaries. A woman who is deeply committed to God may long for her husband to demonstrate spiritual leadership in the home and do a slow disgruntled burn if he fails to do so.

No interest in knowing and being known. Here's a tough one. Your spouse may be the Rock of Gibraltar when it comes to stability, honesty, and integrity. But for whatever reason he or she may have no desire to go deeper with you into sharing thoughts and feelings, to engage in (to quote Dallas Willard again) the "mutual mingling of souls." Indeed, your spouse may be incapable of doing so. If you long for this connection and your spouse isn't willing or able to fulfill it, what do you do? (This is a common scenario in the counseling office, by the way, often coming to the front burner after the children are grown and gone. Many couples wait far too long before they address this issue.)

The next several reasons for disillusionment involve some deeper water, where more than an attitude adjustment will be needed to cope. In fact, you may need to enlist the advice of a medical professional, marriage therapist, and/or counseling pastor to help you navigate through any of these issues because decisive action may be required.

Emotional turbulence. Before you set the wedding date, you may not have paid much attention to your sweetheart's short fuse when he got frustrated or her sulking when things didn't go her way. When you said "I do," you may not have anticipated that your spouse might one day develop a clinical depression or an anxiety disorder or even a full-blown psychosis sometime in the future. Can you stay the course when this occurs?

Character issues. How do you feel when you discover that your spouse doesn't always tell the truth? What if she loves to gossip? What if his initiative faded away soon after he left college? What if she flirts with other men? What if he can't keep his cursor away from Internet porn sites?

Destructive communications. As we've noted elsewhere in this book, the verbal assaults that spouses hurl at each other often overshadow whatever were the original issues between them. Dealing with the disillusionment and betrayal generated by these injuries and learning more appropriate ways to manage disagreements often represent the first (and prolonged) order of business in marriage counseling.

Addictions. Alcohol abuse. Dependency on prescription drugs or street drugs. Gambling. Compulsive shopping. Overeating. Pornography. Addictions are destructive and discouraging. They also involve lying to everyone in general, and especially to a spouse. True intimacy, knowing and being known, is impossible in the face of an ongoing addiction. What do you do when you realize that your spouse is enslaved to some substance or activity? That you are an addict? That you both are addicts?

When your spouse is an addict

Addictions of all kinds (alcohol, street or prescription drugs, pornography, gambling, eating, spending) by their very nature cause a severe disruption in communication between the spouses. The denial and lying that are routinely needed to maintain an addiction directly undermine intimacy between two people. Denial involves working hard to lie to yourself, and if you can't tell yourself the truth, how can you begin to tell the truth to your partner?

Intimacy grows when sharing takes place on a deep level. If I bare my heart to you on an issue that's troubling me, and you listen with unfeigned interest and compassion, I'm drawn to you. I trust you because you've listened intently without trying to fix me, change my mind, or discount my feelings. The addict can't share her deepest feelings, because doing so would put a spotlight on the elephant in the room: the fact that the addiction is a source of both shame and disintegration and needs to be eradicated. If an addict isn't ready for change, she won't "go there" with her husband. If he doesn't know about the addiction, he will still sense emotional withholding and unavailability from his wife. Efforts to promote intimacy will be met with resistance, and dissatisfaction will grow like a cancer in the relationship.

If a spouse *does* know about the other's addiction and isn't taking serious action to confront it, the nonaddicted spouse may be getting some traction from being on the moral high ground in the relationship. Teri worked with a couple in which an alcoholic husband finally quit drinking. His wife had spent nearly two decades focused on her role as the long-suffering spouse of the hard-drinking bad boy. As he successfully maintained his sobriety, he climbed out of the shame pit long enough to identify some serious issues in her behavior (most notably her own addiction to shopping). She fell apart as he began (quite properly) to express his concerns in the counseling office. Sensing that her position of moral superiority was being threatened, she began to undermine his recovery process.

A more common scenario is one in which the addiction is causing all sorts of havoc, and no one is ready to address it. In

(continued)

fact, spouse, children, and other family members may be accommodating the addict and shielding him from the consequences of his behavior (a pattern known as *enabling*). The details of the process of taking the addiction bull by the horns will depend on the type of problem and the options available to the spouse and family.

We won't attempt to dive into that process here,[1] except to note that at some point a loving confrontation (some use the term *carefrontation*) will be necessary. This will require careful planning with the assistance of one or more people who are experienced in this type of situation. It will involve, most of all, telling the truth: how much the addict is loved; how the addiction is affecting spouse, family, and friends (not to mention the addict herself); how enabling is going to stop immediately; what step(s) the addict is being asked to take; and what will happen if she doesn't cooperate. This last component, the "or else" of the discussion, must be carefully thought out and cannot be an idle threat. If a spouse intends to begin a time of separation if the addict won't play ball, for example, there had better be a place already lined up for that contingency.

There are two more causes for disillusionment that will require specific and definitive action on the part of a spouse:

Infidelity. An emotional and/or physical liaison with someone outside of the marriage represents a major breach in loyalty and trust, a rip in the hull of the marital ship of state. It cannot be ignored. The damage can be repaired—indeed, an authentic repair can actually lead to a deeper intimacy than the couple has known before—but not without *a lot* of effort.

Restoring a marriage after one or both partners have been unfaithful is an arduous process, one that is more complex than we can set forth here. Needless to say, individual and couple's counseling, accountability, and a gradual restoration of trust will be needed over months or even years before the marriage is restored. The bad news is that a true repair (which requires going all the way down to bedrock) is really long, hard work. The good news is that the marital bond may be stronger than it ever was before, once this process has been completed.

Abuse. Physical, verbal, emotional, sexual abuse—all of it violates the wedding vows and common decency. Sadly, some spouses remain on the receiving end for years before they acknowledge these assaults as inappropriate, evil, and dangerous. For the victim of abuse, conducting oneself to safety (along with any children, if they are in harm's way) is the first and immediate priority.

This one's really simple in some ways, and terribly complex in others. The main concern isn't so much disillusionment as it is safety. Physical or sexual abuse of a spouse or children is grounds for immediate separation, period. Safety is the most important immediate concern, and usually it's not possible to be safe from an abuser until one is out of his reach. Usually the perpetrator of physical and/or sexual abuse is a male, but not always. Verbal abuse, on the other hand, is an equal-opportunity transgression.

Restoring a marriage to an abuser may be impossible, but if

reconciliation is to occur the abuse must stop and there must be adequate safeguards for the victim(s) to be protected from any further harm. This applies to verbal abuse as well, which may not leave physical scars, but can inflict serious emotional and marital damage.

Moving beyond disillusionment

Before we make some specific suggestions regarding what to do about disillusionment, we need to issue seven—count 'em—seven very important "now hear this" reminders about marriage. Sorry if we sound like a couple of drill sergeants here, but we need your full attention at this point. Besides, you won't hear many messages like these from our current culture.

"Now hear this" no. 1: When you got married you took a solemn vow. If you still have a copy of your wedding vows, go back and read them a few times. You made promises to love, honor, cherish, and hang in there with your spouse until death, no matter what. Were you serious or just kidding? Did you consciously make a real body-on-the-line commitment or just utter some vague intentions, subject to repeal without notice?

"Now hear this" no. 2: You may have fallen in love based on how good the other person made you feel (see chapter 1), but marriage isn't about *you* anymore. It's about what you're willing to do for the other person. Believe it or not, it isn't your spouse's job to make you happy.

"Now hear this" no. 3: Since it isn't your spouse's job to make you happy, having your own act together is a crucial part of having a good marriage. You may need to do a whole lot of work on yourself (includ-

ing some counseling, if needed) before you're in a position to address whatever issues you might have with your spouse.

"Now hear this" no. 4: It is very, very, very unusual for marital discord to involve one person who is a saint and another who is a total jerk. If your marriage hasn't turned out the way you'd like, the beginning of wisdom is to take a fearless inventory of your contribution to the problem. (However, even you contributied to a marital mess, that is *not* grounds for being abused.)

"Now hear this" no. 5: Marriages are the soil in which the next generation is grown. No government program or social-service infrastructure can remotely accomplish what takes place in a family built on a solid marriage.

"Now hear this" no. 6: God cares a whole lot about the integrity of marriage. If you're considering violating your marriage vows because someone other than your spouse appears to be more appealing, you are literally squaring off against the Creator of the universe. While we understand there are circumstances in which one has little choice but to end a marriage (such as ongoing physical abuse or repeated, unrepentant infidelity), this step isn't to be taken lightly. Consider the following passage from the last book of the Old Testament, written by the prophet Malachi. (Though he's addressing husbands, wives who break faith with their spouses are also in the crosshairs of this passage.)

> You flood the LORD's altar with tears. You weep and wail because
> he no longer pays attention to your offerings or accepts them with
> pleasure from your hands. You ask, "Why?" It is because the LORD
> is acting as the witness between you and the wife of your youth,

because you have broken faith with her, though she is your partner, the wife of your marriage covenant.

  Has not the LORD made them one? In flesh and spirit they are
his. And why one? Because he was seeking godly offspring. So
guard yourself in your spirit, and do not break faith with the wife
of your youth.

  "I hate divorce," says the LORD God of Israel.[2]

And all God's people said . . . "Yikes!"

"Now hear this" no. 7: Since you and your spouse are both flawed
human beings, where in the world are each of you going to find complete safety, acceptance, loyalty, and abiding love when your faults are
fully on display? Not at the workplace, or on the Internet, or at Starbucks, or on the softball team. Apart from God Himself, your marriage provides the best possible setting for this incredible treasure to be
found. *It's definitely worth the effort to make it all that it can be.*

The invitation

Sadly, far too often an individual's or a couple's response to disillusionment is to declare the marriage unfixable and then abandon ship. We
have seen far too many unhappily married people contact a divorce
lawyer long before they have tried some strategies that often bring major
improvements on the home front.

  We are now going to describe a general approach that we call "the
invitation," which can be applied to a variety of situations that a spouse
might want to address. These can range from course corrections—a

desire to change eating habits, for example—to more serious issues, such as a spouse's emotional weather. (As we just noted, abuse, infidelity, or addictions require a more decisive response that should be coordinated with a counselor and other resources.)

Let's say you're not satisfied with your marriage at this point because of _____ (fill in the blank). *Things aren't what I had hoped and expected. You've changed since the wedding day, and I don't like a lot of what I'm seeing. I've changed, and you don't know what's going on inside me. This isn't what I signed on for.* And so on. What do you do? Soldier on, shut up, and hope that something changes? Nag your spouse? Talk to your friends (*My wife doesn't understand me* or *You won't believe what he said to me last night*)? Bury yourself in your work? Look for someone better? Drown your sorrows in _____ (diversions, whether harmful or constructive)? File for divorce?

Obviously we would hope for a better outcome than any of these. Here are some steps Teri utilizes in the counseling office on a regular basis:

1. Take careful stock of your own responsibility for the disillusionment you may be feeling. Do you expect your spouse to be Superman or Wonder Woman? Do you believe that your spouse is supposed to meet all of your needs and make you happy 24-7? Are you dealing with some physical, emotional, or spiritual disturbances of your own? Assuming that there's a genuine reason for dissatisfaction with the other person's behavior, are you partly responsible because you've gone with the flow for years rather than doing the hard work of seeking changes without nagging? Have you given up on the other person without giving him or her a chance to change (or even hear what your spouse is thinking about)?

2. While you're at it, take careful stock of your spouse's strengths. Before you were married you were probably preoccupied with your beloved's positive attributes. Sadly, all too often we forget to look for them, let alone make a point of acknowledging them to the other person, within a few months after the wedding. If you're dissatisfied with your marriage for whatever reason, it may be very tempting to turn a dark corner in which you begin building your case against your spouse. We all have a host of behaviors that could be considered endearing or annoying depending on the spin the other person decides to put on them.

When our kids were in high school and out at night with their friends, Paul would usually lie awake until he knew they were safely in the door. Teri could have viewed this either as a flaw (being overprotective) or a virtue (watching out for the kids' safety). Her take was actually something in between: "Since he lies awake worrying about them, I don't have to. *Zzzzz.*"

Most character traits aren't inherently good or bad in and of themselves. Rather, they serve a person (and the person's spouse) well in some situations and not so well in others. For example, a husband's tendency to establish a protective hedge against future trouble may drive his wife crazy if he's spending money on asteroid-collision insurance when she wants new carpet. But that very same trait may benefit her when her husband carefully plans a 25th anniversary trip to England, allowing her to relax and know that a comfortable hotel room, reserved weeks in advance, awaits at the end of each day.

Obviously, if you scrutinize anyone carefully enough—which is inevitable when you live together—you can find plenty of things to criticize, especially if you're bent on finding fault. But is all you discover about your spouse after the wedding necessarily negative? As you watch your spouse navigate through some challenges and struggles— perhaps a few that you were responsible for—you may discover character strengths you couldn't have anticipated during your courtship. These need to be kept in mind as you consider what you want to see change.

3. *Figure out what you want or need from the other person.* This may take some time. Indeed, it may take a *lot* of time to sort out. You should start journaling what's on your mind, not only to help collect your thoughts, but also to lay the groundwork for what you might say in your invitation. You should pray earnestly and often. You should seek counsel from a mature friend, a couple with a stable marriage, a pastor, a counselor, or all of the above. In the counseling office, Teri often spends multiple sessions over several weeks on this step. Why does this take time? Because it may not be that clear what is bothering you, let alone what steps you might be asking your spouse to take. All too often an unsuspecting spouse is suddenly confronted with an impossible demand ("I'm unhappy with our marriage—something's got to be done!") or a devastating blindside (divorce papers). This type of abrupt action is not only unfair, but it may also torpedo what might have been a satisfactory repair had the issue been framed properly.

4. *Consider carefully how you might express what you want as one or more specific requests that are realistic.* "I would like to set some specific times to talk about how we manage our finances" is a reasonable request. "I want you to make more money so that we can get out of this dump" isn't. If your spouse is in a perpetually irritable mood, will it be enough to open a dialogue about what's bothering him or her? Should

counseling or a doctor's appointment be on the agenda? Would there be a time frame on that course of action?

5. *Extend an invitation to work on the issue(s) in as warm and generous terms as possible.* "I think we can make this better. Would you be willing to join me? Here is what I'm proposing . . ." Your invitation may have to be scripted very carefully, especially if you have some strong emotion about the issue in question or if you're dealing with one or more character traits. (This is another step in the process that Teri often takes time to map out carefully in the counseling office.) Whether the invitation is given in a letter, at Starbucks, or in the counseling office will depend on your particular situation. If you're worried about being verbally outgunned in a direct conversation, putting your thoughts in writing may be the best option. (Writing out the invitation is a good idea, by the way, even if you intend to present your invitation in person. Doing so helps you clarify your thoughts.)

Beware of issuing an ultimatum, which should be reserved for situations (such as addictions or ethical lapses) in which no isn't an acceptable answer. However, your spouse needs to understand that your concerns are important and shouldn't be waved off. Also, think carefully about the setting for this conversation. If it isn't going to occur in the counseling office, choose a time and place in which you won't be tired or distracted. However, don't put off the process indefinitely because you're worried about your spouse's reaction or you're not sure you want to do the work needed to bring about meaningful change.

6. *The invitation will usually need to include both an acknowledgment of wounds that have been inflicted and a desire to heal them.* Along with whatever specific issues are generating disillusionment, verbal wounds

that have been inflicted over the years will need to be addressed. (Indeed, they may be the primary issue.) So often the original subject(s) of a couple's marital turbulence is (or are) completely overshadowed by the verbal (or even physical) slings and arrows that have been unleashed over months and years of conflict. These must be acknowledged as part of the invitation and may in fact be an extended first order of business before any other issues are addressed.

7. *If the spouse's response is positive ("Where do I sign?" "What should I do?"), great!* You've just taken step one. Now get to work with the process of ongoing conversations, accountability, and counseling (if that's part of the process) to bring about change. Be sure to express your appreciation for your spouse's willingness to join you in this process. If it goes well, be prepared to hear from your spouse about some things that he or she would like to address as well. (This is a good thing, by the way.)

What if the answer to your invitation is no?

What if your spouse says, in so many words, "I like things the way they are. I like myself the way I am, and I'm not interested in your proposal"? What if your spouse sees you, the one making the invitation, as needing change? At this point you have to decide where the dividing line lies between an acceptable and an unacceptable situation. If there is still good and stable stuff in place and the marriage isn't abusive or intolerable in some other way, you'll need to make a conscious commitment to adjust your attitude. If you keep trying to get something that your spouse isn't able to provide, and you remain constantly irritated over what your marriage partner doesn't bring to the table, he or she is only going to become more miserable. (You will too.) Accept what is likely to be "as good as it gets," and be grateful for what your spouse *does* bring to the marriage and your home. You may in so doing bring out the more angelic side of his or her nature. It comes down to respect—for your spouse, for your vows, for the God who invented marriage in the first place.

Teri has observed that—sadly—it's all too common to hear a no answer when the invitation is for more soul-to-soul intimacy in the marriage. This is often a heart-wrenching situation. After decades of faithfully rearing a family and/or earning a living, one person begins to recognize and articulate a deep desire to go to a deeper level of heart and mind with the marriage partner. But when asked to join the adventure of knowing and being known, the other spouse may not have a clue what this is about, or what it feels like. The whole idea may sound unnecessary, frivolous, or even risky. *No thanks . . .* Now what?

When Teri deals with this or other situations in which a spouse's answer to an invitation for change has been a clear no, she will usually offer the disappointed person the following advice in so many words: This may be hard to accept, but you need to quit demanding what your spouse can't or won't give you. Instead, figure out one or more responsible and moral avenues in which your need(s) can be met. This may involve building friendships with other people (of the same gender), investing in the lives of your children or grandchildren, engaging in a ministry to those less fortunate, volunteering for community service, going back to school, joining a book club, and so on. You need to release your anger and your tendency to judge your spouse, no matter how deserving of your wrath you think he or she might be. Indeed, getting your needs appropriately met elsewhere is more likely to help you become less irritated and dissatisfied and actually become more generous with your spouse. It also lowers your risk for having an affair, which at some point may appear to be an attractive option if the "right" person happens to show up on your radar.

Let's pause here for station identification. This is WHOA and WHOA-FM, and here's an important public-service announcement. If you issue an invitation to your spouse to work on some much-desired changes and you hear a no, whether soft or resounding, consider yourself highly vulnerable to infidelity. All too often a sympathetic "friend," manages to show up just when you're in the thick of this sort of rough patch with your spouse. But exercising the affair option only puts you on a fast track to a disaster like few others. If you feel yourself pulled toward someone else's orbit and if you start entertaining "wouldn't it be loverly" thoughts about spending days and nights with that person, and even if you suppose that doing so would be justified in light of your spouse's current lack of appeal, we can only echo what young Jenny yelled to Forrest Gump: "Run, Forrest, run!"*

And now back to our program in progress. There's another important step to take if you intend to meet one or more needs outside of the marriage: Your spouse should be given a clear and gracious message about what you are doing—"I have a need to _____, as we've discussed, and I'd very much like to have you join me in that process. However,

---

* *Forrest Gump*, directed by Robert Zemeckis (Paramount Pictures, 1994). The New Testament expands on the thought of running, as opposed to staying in close proximity to the attractive person and trying to resist the urge to take the next step: "Flee from sexual immorality. All other sins a man commits are outside his body, but he who sins sexually sins against his own body" (1 Corinthians 6:18).

if you don't want to do it with me, I won't nag or be angry with you, but I may need to find what I'm looking for through time spent with other people. I don't want you to be caught by surprise or think that I'm abandoning you. I want to be aboveboard, respect you, and honor our marriage in this process, but this is important enough to me that I plan to take some specific steps. And, yes, this will mean that I'll be investing some time and energy outside of our marriage. However, my overall desire is to enhance our marriage, not undermine it. Here's what I think this will look like . . ."

The reception you receive may range from vague indifference to fierce opposition. You shouldn't be surprised if your spouse is at least a little wary of the whole idea. If your spouse is insecure, you may need to offer ongoing reassurance that you're not looking for a replacement. If he or she has control issues, your proposal may sound very threatening to the status quo and be met with considerable resistance. You may run into a tacit assent followed by a lot of subtle foot dragging and disapproval. ("You're going to your book club *again* tonight? What am I supposed to do for dinner?") Come what may, you should be willing to carry out whatever you're doing with absolute transparency. As soon as you cross into the realm of secrets or anything less than full disclosure, major trust issues will eclipse whatever benefit you might be deriving from the relationships or activities you've sought out.

Keeping dis-illusion from becoming disillusion

We said at the outset of this chapter that some degree of disillusionment is inevitable in any close relationship, and that healthy dis-illusion is necessary for a truly satisfying marriage. Nothing binds one person to another more powerfully than feeling truly safe—fully known, warts and all, yet steadfastly loved and appreciated over the long haul and through the changes life brings. In case you hadn't noticed, this idea has been the centerpiece of our book, and everything we've said up to this point has been written with a fervent desire that we might help couples experience it.

Partly as a recap and partly as a ribbon and bow for this book, we want to offer these reminders:

- Remember that marriage is about what you have promised to do for the other person, not about how good your spouse makes you feel.
- Keep listening and talking to God.
- Keep listening and talking to your spouse.
- Notice the order of the gerunds (the words ending in "-ing" in the previous two statements): Listen first. Don't just listen, but *hear* your spouse.
- Listen to yourself (keep a journal of what you're thinking about, not what you had for breakfast).
- Keep working on yourself—spiritually, emotionally, physically.
- Be realistic and gracious about your spouse's shortcomings.
- Be realistic and gracious about your own shortcomings.
- Apologize to and ask forgiveness from God and your spouse as often as necessary.
- Be fully present in your conversations with your spouse.
- Be fully present in the other parts of your life—savor the moment.

- Ruthlessly eliminate hurry from your life.
- Your spouse isn't the person you married, so make sure you know who he or she has become and is becoming.

Exercise: The painful questions that lead to renewal

1. When you married, what were your assumptions about what marriage would provide you?
2. Look at the section "What can contribute to disillusionment?" Have any of these issues been a negative influence in your ability to have an emotionally intimate relationship with your spouse?
3. What responsibility do *you* take for whatever disillusionment has been experienced in your marriage?
4. What strengths does your spouse have? How do you show appreciation for those qualities?
5. What do you most want from your spouse right now? Have you ever asked for that in a setting that doesn't involve anger or sarcasm?
6. When was the last time you genuinely apologized to your spouse?

Endnotes

1. See also Focus on the Family's *Complete Guide to Family Health, Nutrition and Fitness* (Tyndale House, 2006) in a chapter titled "Bad Habits."
2. Malachi 2:13–16.

Coda

As you drive off into the sunset, you would do well to listen to two songs that beautifully express what we've been striving to say in this book.

Teri's pick: Carly Simon's "The Stuff That Dreams Are Made Of" offers some eloquent encouragement for a woman to look for the hero of her dreams in her own husband. Key lines: "What if the prince on the horse in your fairytale / Is right here in disguise?"[1]

Paul's pick: Andrew Peterson's incredible CD *Love and Thunder*[2] contains the sweet and moving "Family Man," the musings of a husband who traded in his Mustang for a minivan. Key lines: "But everything I had to lose came back a thousand times in you / . . . . And you help me stand 'cause I am a family man."

Endnotes

1. Carly Simon, "The Stuff That Dreams Are Made Of," *Reflections*, copyright (c) 1987, C'est Music, Inc.
2. Andrew Peterson, "Family Man," *Love and Thunder*, copyright (c) 2003, Provident Music. *Love and Thunder* should be heard the first time straight through, start to finish, without distractions.

Appendix 1: Change in the Blended Family

For a substantial number of couples, the process of creating a new civilization involves much more than two people coming to understand each other's backstory and traditions. More than 40 percent of all marriages are actually remarriages for one or both parties, and approximately one in three Americans is a step-something: stepparent, stepchild, stepsibling, or other member of a stepfamily. If you're in a marriage that includes one or more children from a previous union, you've no doubt realized that creating a new civilization under these circumstances is anything but a *Brady Bunch* walk in the park. For one thing, you were probably unable to protect that all-important first year of your marriage even if you were aware that doing so would be a wise idea. More important, a number of complications usually conspire to undermine the formation of your new civilization, whether or not you're aware of them.

Many who remarry often face a more difficult challenge. If they've been badly burned in a previous relationship, they may keep their cards close to the chest and their emotional chips guarded, not quite allowing themselves to believe wholeheartedly that this new marriage will pan out and go the distance. As a result, they keep one foot in the old civilization ("just me and the kids") and one foot in the new ("all of us together like the Brady Bunch").

At the risk of sounding presumptuous, we might paraphrase Genesis 2:24 for them: "For this reason a man will leave his father and mother, as well as his children from his previous marriage, and be united to his wife." Neither the original verse nor our rendition of it would imply that relationships with parents, or existing children, are to be terminated. But both versions make it clear that the marriage relationship takes priority over all others, that marrying someone means going "all in." It's not a decision to be made lightly—all the chips are on the line—but it represents the relational investment that truly yields long-term payoffs.

It's sad but true that conflict surrounding kids is the most common reason blended families don't blend. The setup for this turbulence isn't terribly mysterious. Divorce is rough on everyone involved, but especially for children (of any age) who experience the dismantling of everything that was predictable and secure in their world. If the child is a firstborn, he or she has usually been promoted to a more adult role, especially if living with a mom who is returning to the workforce. Just about the time the child begins to adjust to a new life and gain some semblance of routine again, the parent begins to date. The new boyfriend or girlfriend usually works overtime to court not just the parent but also the kids. Often it's all fun and games until it becomes apparent that a new marriage may be in the works. Caught up in the joy of finding someone with whom to share love again, the parent may become mystified and frustrated by a child's apparently irrational reactions to this turn of events. But from the child's point of view, Mom's or Dad's decision to remarry nearly always represents a collection of major losses:

Loss of the partner role. After a divorce an eldest or only child often assumes the role of a surrogate partner, especially when spending a lot of time with the opposite-sex parent (i.e., sons with moms, daughters with dads). A new stepparent not only bumps the son or daughter back to child status but also assumes the numero-uno position in the parent's affections. The child who is demoted to numero "whatever-o" feels confused and even abandoned—again—as a result.

Loss of a remarriage fantasy. Most kids (especially the younger ones) hold on to a fantasy, conscious or otherwise, that Mom and Dad are miraculously going to mend their differences and remarry. While a parent's new dating relationships may offer some appealing experiences and gifts as fringe benefits, a parent's marrying someone else strikes a fatal blow to the dream of a *Parent Trap*–type of happy reunion.

Loss of feelings of loyalty. Even if children aren't harboring a secret longing to see their parents get back together, the prospect of Mom or Dad having a new partner can put them in a terrific bind: Does friendliness with Mom's new husband constitute disloyalty to the biological dad? If Dad walked out on Mom, doesn't she deserve the sympathy vote—especially if Dad is getting serious with someone else? These questions will be tough whether the relationship with the other parent is shaky or fiercely loyal. They are particularly difficult for a younger child who may not be able to identify and verbalize the conflict, and who may respond by acting out in ways that are bewildering to everyone. (If a child feels insecure with one parent, he or she may create havoc for the other parent's new spouse as an ongoing and unconscious campaign to garner parental approval.)

Loss of the original civilization. The new civilization that is created by merging two existing families often results in loss of status and privileges for the children involved. For example, unless Mom or Dad "remarry up," financially speaking, a child may now have to share a room with a relative stranger, which can feel like a shocking loss of privacy, especially for an adolescent. A child who may have been a first-born or last-born child (with all the perks that go along with those positions) may find him- or herself shifted to a less strategic position in the new lineup. A "baby" daughter who has long become used to the nonstop smiling approval befitting her status as the cute youngster of the family may find herself asking, *What am I, chopped liver?* when a "new" and younger daughter suddenly appears on the scene.

Loss of healthy parental limits: Most parents feel guilty watching their kids suffer through a divorce, even if it involved circumstances beyond their control (such as abandonment). A single parent often relaxes the disciplinary reins with a child in an effort (conscious or otherwise) to compensate for all the pain and tough adjustments, and after a remarriage the biological parent almost always tends to be more lenient than the stepparent when enforcing limits on his or her own kids. After the honeymoon, which has probably been too short or even nonexistent, the stepparent becomes increasingly exasperated that the biological parent isn't imposing appropriate limits with his or her own child. As the irritation evolves into vocal criticism, Mama Bear or Papa Lion will rear up and bare some teeth to protect the cubs from the dangerous intruder. The child, who is now thoroughly disenchanted with the newcomer, senses the brewing storm and figures, *Hey, now's my chance to get rid of this jerk and get my life back again!* (This isn't usually a conscious game plan for a younger child. However, Teri has dealt with several situations in which teenagers from both camps in the blended family have coolly verbalized in private therapy sessions their intentional strategy to create discord with the stated goal of torpedoing the new marriage.)

Loss of consistent discipline. For most children who are living in a remarriage household, the new situation represents the third time they have had to adjust to new rules based on multiple (and rarely consistent) sets of adult authority: the original marriage, the single parent(s), and now the parent and his or her new spouse. It's little wonder that kids pose the greatest challenge to a remarriage. It's hard enough to train them to comply with one set of household rules, let alone several. Receiving new marching orders from yet another adult will hardly produce an enthusiastic response in a child who already feels displaced and disgruntled.

Household rules

Speaking of household rules, we would suggest that you consider the following guidelines if you're creating a new civilization that includes any stepchildren:

1. *Don't have too many lofty expectations about the amount of actual parenting you'll do with stepchildren who are 11 or older.* With few exceptions, the biological parent needs to be the one in charge of his or her own adolescent child(ren). The stepparent should assume a role more like a camp counselor—someone who is to be respected but not intent on barking orders in all directions.

If the other person's child is younger than 11, you *might* have more of a chance to parent that child, especially if you and your spouse have primary custody and if the noncustodial parent isn't highly involved.

Developmentally, younger children are more likely to crave the stability of a cohesive family unit. They haven't yet experienced the adolescent yearning for separation and are more receptive to forming a bond with a new parent.

2. Decide together what the ground rules for all *of the kids in the blended family will be.* The stepparent has the right to expect respectful treatment from any and all stepchildren, but disciplinary measures normally should be enforced by the biological parent.

3. If at all possible, avoid moving into one or the other's existing home. Otherwise, one family may feel like their territory has been invaded, and the other may feel like interlopers in someone else's home. If kids now need to share rooms, ask whom they would prefer as a roommate.

4. Openly acknowledge the problems inherent in blending two civilizations. Hold regular family meetings on a weekly basis, and then eventually monthly. The agenda for these gatherings should include a frank admission of the daunting task both families are undertaking, and then a time to ask, "What's working?" and "What's not working?"

5. Do everything you can to promote a healthy relationship with the noncustodial parent. You may have decided to extricate yourself from a relationship with your former spouse, but your child didn't necessarily make that choice. It's in his or her best interests to have as good a relationship as possible with *both* parents.

6. Don't assume that families can or should blend quickly. In a best-case scenario, it will take a minimum of a year for children to adjust to the new arrangements. Every holiday, birthday, and vacation will have to be done differently now that more people are involved, and negotiating through all of these occasions can be tense.

FOCUS ON THE FAMILY®

Welcome to the Family

Whether you purchased this book, borrowed it, or received it as a gift, we're glad you're reading it. It's just one of the many helpful, encouraging, and biblically based resources produced by Focus on the Family® for people in all stages of life.

Focus began in 1977 with the vision of one man, Dr. James Dobson, a licensed psychologist and author of numerous best-selling books on marriage, parenting, and family. Alarmed by the societal, political, and economic pressures that were threatening the existence of the American family, Dr. Dobson founded Focus on the Family with one employee and a once-a-week radio broadcast aired on 36 stations.

Now an international organization reaching millions of people daily, Focus on the Family is dedicated to preserving values and strengthening and encouraging families through the life-changing message of Jesus Christ.

Focus on the Family MAGAZINES

These faith-building, character-developing publications address the interests, issues, concerns, and challenges faced by every member of your family from preschool through the senior years.

FOCUS ON THE FAMILY THRIVING FAMILY™ Marriage & parenting	FOCUS ON THE FAMILY CLUBHOUSE JR.™ Ages 4 to 8	FOCUS ON THE FAMILY CLUBHOUSE® Ages 8 to 12	FOCUS ON THE FAMILY CITIZEN® U.S. news issues

For More INFORMATION

ONLINE:
Log on to
FocusOnTheFamily.com
In Canada, log on to
FocusOnTheFamily.ca

PHONE:
Call toll-free:
800-A-FAMILY
(232-6459)
In Canada, call toll-free:
800-661-9800

Rev. 10/09

More Great Resources
from Focus on the Family®

Your Marriage Masterpiece
Discovering God's Amazing Design for Your Life Together
by Al Janssen

Like a long-forgotten work of art, marriage is often undervalued and unappreciated. *Your Marriage Masterpiece* takes a fresh look at the exquisite design God has for your marriage and brings to light the reasons your union was intended to last a lifetime. Throughout this creative and refreshing book, you will examine those elements, such as passion, adventure, and commitment, that make a marriage a masterpiece. You will be reminded of God's love and passion for you and your spouse and discover new ways to reflect God's vibrant masterpiece within your marriage.

No More Headaches
Enjoying Sex & Intimacy in Marriage
by Dr. Juli Slattery

As a psychologist and speaker, Dr. Juli Slattery has listened to countless wives tearfully share their hurt and disappointment about their sexual relationships with their husbands. She understands their struggles and the bewilderment they feel. In *No More Headaches*, Juli offers honest answers to the questions wives are afraid to ask. With warmth and compassion, she helps women understand the sexual differences between men and women and offers practical advice for those who want to strengthen—or save—their marriages.

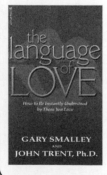

The Language of Love
How to Be Instantly Understood by Those You Love
by Gary Smalley and John Trent, Ph.D.

The frustration of missing out on meaningful communication affects not only our marriages but also our friendships and parent-child and professional relationships. Gary Smalley and John Trent deliver a time-tested method that enables us to bridge communication gaps, opening the door to greater intimacy and lasting change!

FOR MORE INFORMATION

Online:
Log on to FocusOnTheFamily.com
In Canada, log on to focusonthefamily.ca.

Phone:
Call toll free: 800-A-FAMILY
In Canada, call toll free: 800-661-9800.

BPZZXP1